THE PROPER CARE OF RABBITS
TW-110

Photography: CLI, Bruce Crook, Marvin Cummings, Isabelle Francais, Michael Gilroy, Glenna M. Huffmon, Horst Mayer, Michael Mettler, Susan C. Miller, Robert Pearcy, David Robinson, The Photo Source, and Louise Van der Meid.

Art: V.D. Kolganov, A.N. Sitchar, F.E. Terletsky, F. Voitov, and V. V. Zotov.

Distributed in the UNITED STATES to the Pet Trade by T.F.H. Publications, Inc., One T.F.H. Plaza, Neptune City, NJ 07753; distributed in the UNITED STATES to the Bookstore and Library Trade by National Book Network, Inc. 4720 Boston Way, Lanham MD 20706; in CANADA to the Pet Trade by H & L Pet Supplies Inc., 27 Kingston Crescent, Kitchener, Ontario N2B 2T6; Rolf C. Hagen Ltd., 3225 Sartelon Street, Montreal 382 Quebec; in CANADA to the Book Trade by Vanwell Publishing Ltd., 1 Northrup Crescent, St. Catharines, Ontario L2M 6P5 ; in ENGLAND by T.F.H. Publications, PO Box 15, Waterlooville PO7 6BQ; in AUSTRALIA AND THE SOUTH PACIFIC by T.F.H. (Australia), Pty. Ltd., Box 149, Brookvale 2100 N.S.W., Australia; in NEW ZEALAND by Brooklands Aquarium Ltd. 5 McGiven Drive, New Plymouth, RD1 New Zealand; in Japan by T.F.H. Publications, Japan—Jiro Tsuda, 10-12-3 Ohjidai, Sakura, Chiba 285, Japan; in SOUTH AFRICA by Lopis (Pty) Ltd., P.O. Box 39127, Booysens, 2016, Johannesburg, South Africa. Published by T.F.H. Publications, Inc.
MANUFACTURED IN THE UNITED STATES OF AMERICA
BY T.F.H. PUBLICATIONS, INC.

t.f.h.

The Proper Care of
RABBITS

Darlene Campbell

A young crossbred rabbit. The results of crossbreeding are unpredictable—and often quite attractive.

636.9332
C187p

Contents

The Rabbit in History

Throughout the ages, the rabbit has not only provided man with food, clothing, and sport, but also this remarkable little animal has managed to survive and multiply under some adverse circumstances. Exactly when the rabbit became domesticated is not known, but several sources are recorded. One authority states that wild rabbits were first kept caged in Africa, while another records that domestication began during the Middle Ages by French monks, who kept them in captivity and selectively bred them. It is known that as far back as 3000 years ago the rabbit was an important food source in Asia and also in European countries (as long as 1000 years ago).

In almost all records dealing with the rabbit, Spain is mentioned. Caves in Spain, dating back to the Stone Age, contain colored pictures of rabbits and hares, along with other animals of that time period, indicating that the rabbit was important to man in prehistoric times. Rabbits have a very ancient fossil record,

All pet rabbits are descendants of the European wild rabbit, which has the scientific name *Oryctolagus cuniculus.* Note how the coloration of this animal creates a camouflage effect.

making them among the most ancient of living mammals of America and Europe. Some fossils of rabbits date back 30 to 40 million years. A sphinx located in Turkey and dating back to 1500 B.C. is standing on the figures of two rabbits.

In early times, the rabbit was prized mainly as a food source. Around 250 B.C., the Romans encouraged the spread of wild rabbits for hunting. But because the little animal so easily adapted to its surroundings, the project boomeranged. The rabbit was so fertile that it proved impossible to control its numbers by hunting.

Below: Skeletal specimen of a rabbit. *Opposite:* Rabbits can be quite curious about their environment.

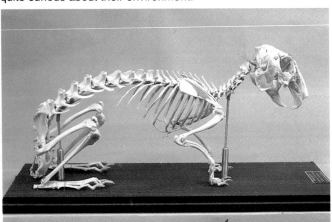

A young male American Fuzzy Lop.

The Portuguese, too, promoted the rabbit as a source of fresh meat on long journeys and experienced the same population problem. Around 1418, Porto Santo (of the Madeira Islands) was literally overrun by rabbits.

The Portuguese had introduced the rabbit to the island, but it multiplied so rapidly and to such an extent that the island had to be abandoned. It was no longer habitable by people.

The rabbit was

In the wild, rabbits subsist mainly on grasses and other vegetation.

introduced into Australia in modern times to provide game for sportsmen, only to have the project end with tragic consequences. European rabbits were set free in the Australian grasslands and, having no natural enemies, they prospered to the extent of competing with herds of livestock for food. Hundreds of miles of grassland were stripped of vegetation. In order to bring the rabbit population under control, predators were introduced. More drastic measures had to be undertaken, and an infectious disease, myxomatosis, was deliberately introduced. Finally, a campaign to destroy the remaining rabbit population on the continent was initiated with the use of poisons.

Another example of the rabbit adapting to its environment was revealed in the latter part of the nineteenth century, when rabbits were released on a group of islands near the South Pole. They were to provide meat for whale hunters and teams of researchers living on the islands. In spite of subarctic temperatures during winter and the complete lack of vegetation, the rabbits managed to survive by eating the seaweed that drifted ashore.

The Romans discovered how to keep the rabbit population under control by raising colonies of them in walled enclosures. The meat was considered a delicacy, and it was believed to contribute to the beauty of a woman. The ancient Aztecs also held the rabbit in esteem for the flavor and quality of its meat. Court physicians prescribed it as an effective body rebuilder, even though they did not realize the scientific value of proteins, carbohydrates, fats, minerals, and vitamins, or that rabbit meat contained these necessary elements for good health in greater degree than did other meats.

The American Indian hunted the wild rabbit in early times, but exactly when the domestic rabbit was introduced in the United States is not known. Since Europeans, especially the French, were fond of rabbit meat—since 1850 over 70 million

Netherland Dwarfs. The small breeds are no less hardy than their larger brothers.

A rabbit with Siamese-type markings. The *points* (ears, nose, tail, and feet) are of a different color than that of the body.

rabbits have been produced annually in France—it is supposed the domestic rabbit was brought into the United States long before 1900.

Americans became rabbit-raising conscious around the turn of the century with the importation of the Belgian Hare, which is not a hare at all, but a rabbit. It was imported from England, and Americans realized that this productive animal was an asset to agriculture.

Rabbitries began springing up across the country, with Los Angeles, California, having more and larger rabbitries than anywhere else in the country. Los Angeles continued to be the major area for rabbit production and processing for many years, and today it still ranks high. This could be due in part to the large population of ethnic groups that consider rabbit a staple in their diet.

The Belgian Hare, with its blockier body than is bred for today and its rapid rate of reproduction, caught the eye of the rabbit-raising public; and a new industry began.

During World War II,
when meat was rationed and extremely difficult to get, rabbit raisers found an eager market for the litters that they could produce in their backyards. People with a few hutches of rabbits soon had a money-making business.

Rabbits are raised in all fifty states and in some United States territories. There are over 40 breeds of rabbit from which you can choose, with numerous varieties within each breed. Most breeds serve a dual purpose: that of meat and fur, or commercial and fancy. Anyone developing an interest in rabbits can be assured that the

Dutch rabbits. Over the years, the rabbit fancy has grown progressively larger as more people have discovered the pleasure and satisfaction of rabbit keeping.

rabbit has been of prime importance to man since the earliest recorded time; and despite adverse circumstances and periodic attempts at eradication, it has survived and flourished and will continue to do so. The rabbit has provided man with a variety of commodities, including meat, pelts, wool, and various by-products. Additionally, it has played an important role in medical research.

With increased knowledge of genetics,

rabbit fanciers have developed a variety of breeds to rival other highly bred animals. The formation of breed clubs has stimulated a spirit of competition, and rabbit exhibitions have sprung up across the country. Anyone can raise rabbits—young or old, retired or employed, man or woman. The endeavor will provide hours of pleasure, relaxation, and an education. It becomes a challenge, and often a hobbyist develops an interest in showing his finest stock at local rabbit shows and county fairs.

Rabbits are not nearly as demanding as are many other kinds of pets.

Why Rabbits?

Millions of domestic rabbits are raised each year. While many people think of the rabbit first as a pet, it is a fact that it has been put to a number of commercial usages. For example, rabbit is used as a source of high-quality meat—at a fraction of the expense of raising beef.

With a 31-day gestation period, a well-maintained doe can raise four to six litters of six to eight fryers in the span of one year. The young rabbits reach four to five pounds, depending upon the breed, and are ready for butchering only 12 to 14 weeks after conception. When dressed out, there is very little loss: 12 to 14 percent. This is 70 to 95 pounds of dressed, edible meat per year, per doe. It takes only one breeding buck for every ten does.

Feed conversion is very good. Using records to verify the cost of maintaining breeding stock and raising the young, the ratio of feed to meat is 4:1. No other animal can be maintained in the small space alloted to a doe and produce eight to ten times its own weight in edible

Many rabbit hobbyists find lop-type rabbits particularly appealing because of their docile, tranquil nature.

A typically alert Netherland Dwarf.

including beef and chicken. Rabbit meat is easily digested, low in cholesterol, and lower in calories than other kinds of meat.

Another demand for rabbits comes from science and medical laboratories. Laboratories use over 600,000 rabbits yearly. They need parasite-free young rabbits of certain weight at specific intervals, depending upon the laboratory. Domestic rabbits play a vital role in producing vaccines and serums for the benefit of mankind. (It should be noted that marketing to laboratories is usually not the aim of the average rabbit hobbyist.)

meat in one year. The nutritional quality of rabbit meat exceeds all other types of meat available on the consumer market,

Rex rabbit. The fur of this attractive breed has the look and feel of velvet.

Pelts are a by-product of meat production. Fur buyers are always in the market for quality pelts (especially white, which is easily dyed), and they have certain guidelines for the condition of the pelts they receive. In some parts of the country, the pelts must be wrapped and shipped to the buyer; while in other areas, the buyer comes to the producer. In areas where trapping of wildlife is legal, fur buyers have pickup points, and the owner of a rabbit herd has a ready outlet for his pelts. The fur is used in the manufacture of toys, novelties, and trim on accessories and clothing. The garment industry purchases from the fur buyer and uses dyed rabbit fur in the place of expensive, exotic furs.

For many rabbit hobbyists, rabbits have

In addition to being a popular pet, the rabbit has been useful to man as a source of meat and fur.

uses far beyond that of their commercial market value. They are delightful pets and are also a means of teaching animal husbandry to youngsters. Gardeners utilize rabbit manure as a source of nitrogen, since it is higher in nitrogen content than any other livestock manure. Earthworms are another source of income to the rabbit raiser: The worms are raised under the cages, turning the manure into a safe, organic potting soil. (There are certain guidelines for this aspect of the hobby as well. So, should you decide to raise earthworms, it is best to visit an earthworm grower beforehand to find out exactly what is involved in such a project.)

Finally, the most important ingredient in raising rabbits is a liking for animals. In choosing to keep rabbits, you can find a pleasant pastime and rewarding hobby.

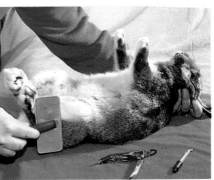

Even though its fur is short, this rabbit is being given a light brushing to remove any loose hair. It also has had its claws clipped.

Selecting a Breed

A breed is a group of animals within a species having common ancestors and certain characteristics that distinguish it from other groups of animals. The characteristics that distinguish one breed from another can be seen in body shape and size; head shape and proportion; ear length, width, and set; and the color pattern, texture, and length of the coat.

The terms *scrub, grade, purebred,* and *registered,* sometimes used when describing the general quality of a rabbit, are defined as follows: A *scrub rabbit* is one unidentifiable as to any specific breed. A *grade rabbit* is one that, although not purebred, is identifiable as to breed. Frequently, a grade rabbit has a purebred sire or dam. A *purebred rabbit* is one that has a pedigree showing ancestors of the same breed for three generations, making it eligible for registration if it meets all physical qualifications required by the registering body. A *registered rabbit* is one that has met all of the qualifications of a given registering body. In the United States, where rabbits are permanently registered

A mixed-breed rabbit feeding on a variety of garden produce.

by means of an ear tattoo, the national rabbit registry is the American Rabbit Breeders Association (ARBA). In Great Britain, where rabbits are registered by the use of leg bands, the national rabbit organization is known as the British Rabbit Council.

BASIC CONSIDERATIONS

Probably the toughest decision that you will have to make is in selecting the one rabbit breed that is most suitable for you, as each of the breeds has its own unique charm and appeal. The best thing for you to do is to first decide what

Pet shops stock rabbit food, grooming tools, and a variety of other items for your pet.

Rex rabbits. There is also a smaller version of this breed, which is known as the Mini Rex.

you want from your rabbit. For example, is the animal to be strictly a pet? Or, do you have intentions of getting involved in the exhibition side of the hobby later on in the future? Are you interested in breeding rabbits? Your answers to these questions can help you in the process of selecting your rabbit. Another consideration is that of fur type, a brief discussion of which follows.

Dutch rabbit. The fur of this breed is classified as normal: it is short and dense.

TYPES OF RABBIT FUR

Rabbit breeds fall into one of four distinct and different fur (or coat) types. The fur type is the basis for the first basic difference between the rabbit breeds.

Normal

The fur common to most rabbits and most familiar to the average person. The characteristic dominant coat has an undercoat protected by longer protective guard hairs.

These youngsters are bringing their new bunny home. The carrier that they are using is a good choice, as it provides ventilation on several sides.

Jersey Wooly. This little rabbit, which was developed by Bonnie Seeley, is the smallest of the wool-rabbit breeds.

Angora

A long coat of wool-type fiber, making it excellent for spinning and weaving. (A variation of this is the Satin Angora coat, which came about from breedings between Satin and Angora-type rabbits.)

Rex

A mutation of the normal coat. This type of fur is shorter and more plush in texture than is normal fur. The guard hairs are reduced in length so as to be nearly the length of the undercoat, presenting a level

Mini Rex. The plush effect of this breed's fur is due to the fact that the length of the undercoat and the length of the guard hairs are nearly the same.

appearance to the coat. Rex fur is very luxurious to the touch.

Satin

This kind of coat is characterized by fine hair shafts. The hair shells, which are more transparent than those of normal-furred rabbits, reflect light. A satin coat exhibits a beautiful satin-like sheen.

There is no best rabbit breed. The one

This is a good way to hold a dwarf-type rabbit. The legs are secured to prevent the animal's jumping and injuring itself.

that the hobbyist feels is most appealing is probably the one best suited to him. One final note on selecting a rabbit: purchase the best rabbit that you can afford. It will be much easier to care for a healthy, well-conditioned rabbit than one that is not in a state of good health.

RABBIT STANDARDS

It goes without saying that for the hobbyist who plans to show his rabbits, a familiarity with the *standard* for his particular breed is a must: a standard is a "picture in words" that describes the ideal breed specimen.

Keep in mind that standards can vary from place to place and from time to time, as they are periodically updated and/or revised. To find out about the standard for your chosen rabbit breed, contact the national rabbit association for the area in which you live.

BREEDS OF RABBIT

The following descriptions are of breeds recognized by the ARBA. Individual clubs are located around the country to support specific breeds and varieties. (These clubs are an excellent means of exchanging information and ideas among rabbit keepers.)

A trio of American Fuzzy Lops. As is true for many of the other rabbit breeds, Fuzzy Lops are available in a wide variety of beautiful colors.

American

VARIETIES: Blue, White

WEIGHT: Bucks 9 to 11 pounds; Does 10 to 12 pounds

The body of the American should exhibit a moderate arch, which begins at the shoulders and reaches its high point in the area just in front of the hip joint. Overall, the American appears compact. It is a rabbit of medium bone and medium weight.

American. This attractive breed was developed in the United States in the early part of the twentieth century.

American Fuzzy Lop. This rabbit exhibits what is known as a *broken pattern,* the coloration of which is white with any other recognized breed color.

American Fuzzy Lop

GROUPS: Agouti, Broken, Pointed White, Self, Shaded, Solid

COLORS: Agouti—Chestnut, Chinchilla, Lynx, Opal, Squirrel; Broken—any recognized breed color along with White and exhibiting the breed pattern; Pointed White—White body with the points of any recognized color; Self—Black, Blue, Chocolate, Lilac; Self (Blue-Eyed Whites and Ruby-

American Sable. When this breed is viewed in reflected light, its brown eyes exhibit a ruby-red glow.

Eyed Whites)—White; Shaded—Sable Point, Siamese Sable, Siamese Smoke Pearl, Tortoiseshell; Solid—Fawn, Orange

WEIGHT: Bucks and Does, not over 4 pounds

The Fuzzy Lop, one of the newer breeds of rabbit, exhibits a body that is cobby and short in appearance. Beginning at the shoulders, there should be good depth that continues back to the hindquarters, which should be well filled and well rounded. The head is set high and close to the shoulders. The Fuzzy Lop is a wool-breed rabbit; its wool should be dense, and the density is, ideally, even throughout the entire body.

American Sable

COLOR: Rich sepia brown on the ears, face, back and outside of legs, and the upper side of the tail. Saddle

The color of the American Sable's fur is a rich shade of sepia brown that varies in intensity on different parts of the animal's body.

Angora, English. This impressive-looking rabbit is distinguished by the tassels and fringes of wool on its head and ears.

color will consistently gradate to a paler tone on the flanks and the underside of the belly and tail.

WEIGHT: Bucks 7 to 9 pounds; Does 8 to 10 pounds

The body is to be of medium length. There is to be good depth and width in the shoulders, as well as the midsection and hindquarters. The American Sable's top line should present itself in an unbroken continuous curve. The hindquarters are to be smooth and well rounded.

Angora (English)

GROUPS: Agouti, Pointed White, Self, Shaded, Solid, Ticked

COLORS: White (Pointed Whites)—White with marking color of Black, Blue, Chocolate or Lilac; Self (Blue-Eyed Whites and Red-Eyed Whites)—White; Colored—Agouti, Chestnut, Chinchilla, Chocolate Agouti, Chocolate Chinchilla, Copper, Lilac Chinchilla, Lynx, Opal, Squirrel, Wild Gray; Self—Black, Blue, Chocolate, Lilac; Shaded—Blue Cream,

French Angora. This rabbit exhibits the erect ear carriage that is also displayed by a number of the other rabbit breeds.

Chocolate Tortoiseshell, Dark Sable, Frosted Pearl, Lilac Cream, Sable, Smoke Pearl, Tortoiseshell; Solid—Cream, Fawn, Red; Ticked—Blue Steel, Chocolate Steel, Lilac Steel, Steel

WEIGHT: Bucks 5 to 7 pounds; Does 5 to 7 ½ pounds

The English Angora has a compact, cobby body with a good uniform coat of wool. It has the appearance of a round ball of fluff. The head has heavy bangs and side trimmings, and the ears are heavily tasseled. The legs, feet, and tail are covered with wool to the extreme ends. The wool of this rabbit is silky in nature. It is, in fact, a wool-producing animal, whereas some other breeds of rabbit are considered to be fur producers.

Angora (French)

GROUPS: Agouti, Pointed White, Self, Shaded, Solid, Ticked

COLORS: White (Pointed Whites)—White with marking color of Black, Blue, Chocolate or Lilac; Self (Blue-Eyed Whites and Red-Eyed Whites)—White; Colored—Agouti, Chestnut, Chinchilla, Chocolate Agouti, Chocolate Chinchilla, Copper, Lilac Chinchilla, Lynx, Opal, Squirrel, Wild Gray; Self—Black, Blue, Chocolate, Lilac; Shaded—Blue Cream, Chocolate Tortoiseshell, Dark

French Angora. This rabbit is a bit larger than its English cousin. Its ears may be plain, or they may have wool tufts on the ends.

Sable, Frosted Pearl, Lilac Cream, Sable, Smoke Pearl, Tortoiseshell; Solid— Cream, Fawn, Red; Ticked—Blue Steel, Chocolate Steel, Lilac Steel, Steel

WEIGHT: Bucks and Does, 7 ½ pounds to 10 ½ pounds

This breed is older than the English Angora and is *the* commercial wool-producing rabbit. A coarse-textured wool grows to an ideal length of 2 ½ to 3 ½ inches. The body is medium in length with a full chest. It is longer and heavier in bone than the English variety. The head is longer and narrower than the English and does not have the heavy bangs and tassels. The tail is covered with wool, but the feet and legs are short-furred to the first joint. The ears may be tufted but not tasseled.

Angora (Giant)

VARIETY: White

WEIGHT: Bucks 8 ½ pounds and over; Does 9 pounds and over

The Giant Angora, considered by some to be one of the most striking of the wool rabbit breeds, should present an overall image of an animal that is well nourished and firmly fleshed. An ideal specimen will be well balanced throughout the body. The density of the wool—the greater, the better—is, ideally, consistently even all over the animal.

Angora (Satin)

GROUPS: Agouti, Pointed White, Self,

Giant Angora. This breed comes only in white. Its head furnishings (the tassels and fringes) are quite abundant.

Shaded, Solid, Ticked
COLORS: White
(Pointed Whites)—White
with marking color of
Black, Blue, Chocolate,
or Lilac; Self (Blue-Eyed
Whites and Red-Eyed
Whites)—White;
Colored—Agouti,
Chestnut, Chinchilla,
Chocolate Agouti,
Chocolate Chinchilla,
Copper, Lilac
Chinchilla, Lynx, Opal,
Squirrel, Wild Gray;
Self—Black, Blue,
Chocolate, Lilac;
Shaded—Blue Cream,
Chocolate Tortoiseshell,
Dark Sable, Frosted
Pearl, Lilac Cream,
Sable, Smoke Pearl,
Tortoiseshell; Solid—
Cream, Fawn, Red;
Ticked—Blue Steel,
Chocolate Steel, Lilac
Steel, Steel
WEIGHT: Bucks and

Satin Angoras. With their silky, shiny coats, these rabbits are truly beautiful animals.

Contrary to the misconception generated by its name, the Belgian Hare is, indeed, a rabbit. It is given credit for increasing the popularity of rabbit-keeping in the United States.

Does, 6 pounds or over

The Satin Angora is of medium length with hindquarters that are well filled. The oval head is to be in balance with the body shape and size. The wool of the Satin exhibits a luxuriant richness in color. Glass-like hair shafts permit the reflection of light.

Belgian Hare

COLOR: Red chestnut

WEIGHT: Bucks and

Head study of a Belgian Hare. The color of this breed is a rich shade of red chestnut.

Does, 6 to 9 ½ pounds

This breed of rabbit originated in Belgium. Some believe it is descended from an early breed known as the Patagonian (the forefather of the Flemish Giant), which is now extinct. It is the race horse of the rabbit family, with a long, streamlined body and a nicely arched back with a sweep that runs continuously from the shoulders to the tail. The loin and hindquarters are well rounded. The body is carried well off the ground on long, straight, slender legs. The head is rather long and fine, set on a slender neck. The fur lies close to the body and is of a rather harsh texture.

Beveren. This large-sized rabbit originated in Beveren, Belgium.

Beveren

VARIETIES: White, Blue, Black

WEIGHT: Bucks 8 to 10 pounds; Does 9 to 11 pounds

The Beveren is one of the rarer breeds in the United States, although it rose in popularity in Europe after its development late in the 19th century.

It is a large breed that produces young that grow rapidly. The body is medium in length and has a meaty back that is slightly arched. The back is full and has good curvature when viewed from the side. The correct color is for the blue to be a clean shade of lavender blue all the way to the skin. The black variety is jet black deep into the fur.

Britannia Petite

COLOR: White

WEIGHT: Bucks and Does, maximum weight of 2 ½ pounds

Small in stature but big in spirit aptly describes the Petite. In general appearance, it is slender and fineboned, with an attractive sleek coat. Members of this breed are known for their alert, inquisitive nature and their lively mannerisms.

Britannia Petite. This diminutive bunny, which comes only in white, is known for its lively, inquisitive nature.

Californian. In an ideal specimen, the color of the nose, ears, feet, and tail will be as black as possible.

Californian

COLOR: White with Black

WEIGHT: Bucks 8 to 10 pounds; Does 8 ½ to 10 ½ pounds

One of the most popular breeds, the Californian was produced for use as an all-purpose commercial rabbit. It excels both as a meat type and a fur type. This is a white rabbit with a colored nose, ears, feet, and tail. The color is to be as black as possible.

Champagne D'Argent. This breed, which originated in the Champagne region of France, has a fur color that is like that of old silver.

The body is very plump and full over the hips, firm and meaty as possible to the nape of the neck and down the sides over the ribs and shoulders.

Champagne D'Argent

COLOR: Silver

WEIGHT: Bucks 9 to 11 pounds; Does 9 ½ to 12 pounds

This is one of the oldest rabbit breeds, having been raised in France for over one hundred years. The pelt commands a high price. The name is French for the "silver rabbit from Champagne," the region where the breed originated. The Champagne is both a commercial and exhibition rabbit. The body is moderate in length, and well developed in the hindquarters, shoulders, and back. The most desirable color is that of old silver, or the pale color of skimmed milk with no hint of yellow. The young of this breed are born black and gradually turn to a velvety silver color once past four months of age.

Checkered Giant (American)

VARIETIES: Black, Blue

COLOR: Black or blue markings on a white background

Checkered Giant. In this breed and many others, the distinctive nose marking is known as a *butterfly.*

Weight: Bucks 11 pounds or over; Does 12 pounds or over

This distinctive breed was derived from the Flemish Giant and is an excellent exhibition rabbit. The first Checkered Giants were imported into the United States in 1910; and since that time, the breed has developed into a distinctive American type. The body is long and well arched, with medium-broad hindquarters. The butterfly across the nose, eye circles, cheek spots, ears, spine marking, tail, and side markings are clear and distinct.

Chinchilla

Chinchilla Breeds: American, Giant, Standard

Color: To be like that of real Chinchilla

Undercolor is dark slate blue at the base, followed by a band of light pearl, followed by a band of black, then a light band ticked with black. Chest is pearl; the belly is white. All three breeds share this distinct color pattern, but each is considered a separate breed.

The Chinchilla produces the highest-priced rabbit pelt in Europe and is a prize exhibition rabbit.

AMERICAN CHINCHILLA: Bred for size, the American is the result of selectively breeding the Standard Chinchilla. It is medium in body length and well rounded in the hips, with well-

A pair of Standard Chinchillas. This breed is the smallest of the three Chinchilla breeds.

filled loin and hips. The back is slightly arched starting at the ear base.

WEIGHT: Bucks 9 to 11 pounds; Does 10 to 12 pounds

GIANT CHINCHILLA: The Giant came about by selective crossbreeding with Flemish Giants. This is the only giant rabbit that is considered

This hefty rabbit is a Giant Chinchilla. The large breed known as the Flemish Giant was used in the development of this breed.

primarily a meat type. The body is large, full in front and hindquarters, with a firm, meaty saddle.

WEIGHT: Bucks 12 pounds and over; Does 13 pounds and over

STANDARD CHINCHILLA: The Standard Chinchilla's body is short and broad. In overall appearance, it appears compact.

WEIGHT: Bucks 5 to 7 pounds; Does 5 ½ to 7 ½ pounds

Cinnamon. Smoke-gray ticking contrasts nicely with the rust or cinnamon color of this breed, which has a medium-long body.

Cinnamon

COLOR: Rust or Cinnamon; a darker color is to be present on all extremities

WEIGHT: Bucks 8 ½ to 10 ½ pounds; Does 9 to 11 pounds

The Cinnamon is a rabbit of medium length. Both its hindquarters and shoulders are well developed. The smooth, well-rounded hindquarters, well filled with flesh, are slightly wider and deeper than the shoulders and

Creme D'Argent. This pretty rabbit is distinguished by the color of its fur, which is a delicate shade of orange. As is required for a number of the other rabbit breeds, the bright eyes should be bold and alert in expression.

should blend into a well-rounded loin and back. The well-shaped head is to be in proportion to the body.

Black Dutch rabbits. The Dutch, which supposedly originated in Holland, is one of the most well-known breeds of rabbit. It is on the small side compared to many of the other rabbit breeds.

Creme D'Argent

COLOR: Creamy orange

WEIGHT: Bucks 8 to 10 ½ pounds; Does 8 ½ to 11 pounds

The Creme D'Argent is similar to the Champagne but is smaller. It has a moderately long body with well-developed hindquarters, deep, thick loins, and broad, well-developed shoulders. The back is slightly arched and tapers toward the shoulders. The color is creamy white with an orange cast. The under-color is bright orange down to the skin.

Dutch

VARIETIES: Black, Blue, Chocolate, Tortoise, Steel, Gray

WEIGHT: Bucks and Does, 3 ½ to 5 ½ pounds

The white area on the front of a Dutch's head is known as a *blaze*. Ideally, it will be medium wide and wedge shaped.

Dwarf Hotot. This breed, which is of German origin, is distinguished by the dark eyebands around the eyes.

The Dutch, which probably originated in Holland, is the popular white rabbit with contrasting "britches." It is strictly a fancy or exhibition rabbit, with a very distinct color pattern. Although small, this breed is meaty, compact, and cobby.

Dwarf Hotot

COLOR: White throughout, except for the eyebands, which are black

WEIGHT: Bucks and Does, 3 ¼ pounds

maximum

The Dwarf Hotot is one of the newer additions to the rabbit fancy. Its body is short, compact, and well rounded. Hindquarters are well rounded, and there is uniform width from shoulders to hips. The head is relatively large, with short, well-furred ears. The distinguishing feature of the breed is the black eyeband that outlines the eye. It should be narrow and uniform,

English Spot. The colored stripe on top of the back is known as a *herringbone* or *spine marking*. The spots that run from behind the ear down the side of the body are known as the *chain markings*.

Balance is a key word when it comes to assessing the markings of the English Spot: both sides of the animal should be marked in the same way.

without any breaks or feathering.

English Spot

VARIETIES: Black, Blue, Chocolate, Gold, Gray, Lilac, Tortoise

COLOR: Colored markings on a white ground

WEIGHT: Bucks and Does, 5 to 8 pounds

This is a very old breed imported from England. The face markings (the butterfly nose, eye circles, and cheek spots) are similar to those of the Checkered Giant. The chain markings on the sides of the body run

Flemish Giant. This breed is aptly named, for it is indeed very large and heavy boned. However, it should be neither flabby nor overly fat.

up to the base of the ears. This chain is a very important part of the breed's markings and should not appear on the Checkered Giant. As an exhibition rabbit, the English Spot's markings are of prime importance—not too few, not too many, not too small, not too large. A good specimen is a breeder's delight.

Flemish Giant

VARIETIES: Steel Gray, Light Gray, Sandy, Black, Blue, White, Fawn

WEIGHT: Bucks 13 pounds or over; Does 14 pounds or over

This is probably one of the most popular of the giant breeds. It has one of the oldest and strongest recognized breed clubs in the United

Florida White. Originally, this breed was developed to be used for research. It is rather on the short side and has pink eyes and pure white fur.

States. The Flemish Giant exhibits a powerful, massive build that is proportioned and well balanced throughout.

Florida White

COLOR: White

WEIGHT: Bucks and Does, 4 to 6 pounds

The Florida White was originally developed for research purposes. This is a rather short rabbit whose shoulders and hindquarters are well developed.The top line of the Florida White should

be one that is curved, rising gradually from ear base to the center of the hips and then curving downward to the tail base. The Florida White has a round, full head, topped by stocky and well-furred ears. Both the head and the ears are to be in balance with the body.

Harlequin

GROUPS: Japanese, Magpie

VARIETIES: Black, Blue,

Harlequins are distinguished by their checkered-pattern coloration. There are two types of Harlequin: Japanese and Magpie.

Chocolate, and Lilac

WEIGHT: Bucks 6 ½ to 9 pounds; Does 7 to 9 ½ pounds

There are two types of Harlequin rabbit: the Japanese and the Magpie. The Japanese variety has its base coat color alternating with bands of orange or its dilute. The Magpie has the basic color alternating with bands of white. This is much the same as a calico cat.

The head is divided in color, one side the base color, the other side the banding color of orange, its dilute, or white. The ears are to be the opposite color for each side, giving a checkered

A pair of Havanas. These small, cobby rabbits sport coats that are soft and lustrous.

The Himalayan, or "Himmy," as it is referred to by some, is long and cylindrical in shape. Older members of this breed sometimes lose some of the richness of their color.

appearance. Also, the legs alternate in color.

Havana

VARIETIES: Blue, Chocolate, Black

WEIGHT: Bucks and Does, 4 ½ to 6 ½ pounds

The Havana is a small meaty rabbit. The body is cobby, with meaty shoulders tapering from slightly broader and higher hindquarters. The rich fur is soft and lustrous with a high sheen.

Himalayan

VARIETIES: Black, Blue

WEIGHT: Bucks and Does, 2 ½ to 4 ½ pounds

One of the world's oldest recognized breeds of rabbit. The coat is snow white with the

Hotot. The eyebands, which are dark black in color, should completely encircle the eyes, which are dark brown.

nose, ears, feet, and tail a rich, velvety black or a rich medium blue at maturity. This is an exhibition rabbit with ruby-red eyes. Fanciers take care not to expose the coat to the sun, as the markings may fade to gray or a rusty brown. Older specimens, too, have a tendency to lose the rich color of this distinctively patterned coat.

Hotot

COLOR: White throughout, except for

the eyebands, which are deep black

WEIGHT: Bucks 8 to 10 pounds; Does 9 to 11 pounds

This breed of rabbit is not quite as well known as are many of the other rabbit breeds. The Hotot's notable characteristic is the deep black band that encircles the eye, providing a striking contrast with the whiteness of the rest of the body.

In conformation, the Hotot is well rounded; its musculation, which is evenly distributed, imparts an impression of strength. An overall compactness is desirable in the breed.

Jersey Wooly. The Netherland Dwarf contributed to the development of this breed. This can be seen in the rounded head and short ears. The Jersey Wooly is a compact little rabbit.

Jersey Wooly

GROUPS: Agouti, Pointed White, Self, Shaded, Tan Pattern

COLORS: Self—Black, Blue Chocolate, Lilac; Self—(Blue-eyed White and Ruby-Eyed White)—White; Shaded—Blue Cream, Sable Point, Seal, Siamese Sable, Smoke Pearl, Tortoise; Agouti—Chestnut Agouti, Chinchilla, Opal, Squirrel; Tan Pattern—Black Otter, Black Silver Marten, Blue Silver Marten, Blue Otter, Chocolate Silver Marten, Lilac Silver Marten, Sable Silver Marten, Smoke Pearl Marten; Pointed (Pointed White)—White

WEIGHT: Bucks and Does, 3 ½ pounds or under

The Jersey Wooly is another of the new wool rabbit breeds. It was developed by Bonnie Seeley. This small rabbit, whose pint-sized stature can be attributed, in part, to crossings with a Netherland Dwarf, sports a dense wool coat. The ears, however, should not have large tufts or tassels; the ends of the ears may carry small tufts.

The Jersey Wooly's overall appearance is one of compactness and good depth.

Lilac

COLOR: Dove-gray with a pinkish tint

WEIGHT: Bucks 5 ½ to 7 ½ pounds; Does: 6 to 8 pounds

The Lilac is a compact breed of rabbit that is robust and energetic in its overall appearance. Other physical qualities

A ruby-eyed white Jersey Wooly.

are those of balance and well roundedness. A good Lilac will radiate a warm glow, due to the pinkish-dove hue of the lustrous fur. In texture, the fur is both dense and soft to the touch.

Lop (English)

GROUPS: Agouti, Brindled, Broken, Self, Shaded, Solid, Ticked

WEIGHT: Bucks 9 pounds and over; Does 10 pounds and over

The body of the

An English Lop. Ear lengths of over 30 inches have been recorded for this breed.

While ear length is important when evaluating this breed, quality and overall balance are even more significant considerations.

English Lop is massive, thick set, and well fleshed. The outstanding feature of this breed is the ears, which, when measured from tip to tip, should be at least 21 inches in length. The English Lop is considered to be one of the oldest domesticated-rabbit breeds. In Europe, it is sometimes referred to as the "King of the Fancy."

Lop (French)

GROUPS: Agouti, Brindled, Broken, Self, Shaded, Solid, Ticked

WEIGHT: Bucks 10 pounds and over; Does 11 pounds and over

The body is of medium length with the back

French Lops. Fanciers of this breed claim that French Lops are very people oriented and that they make wonderful pets.

well arched and the head carried low. In showing this breed, the ear carriage and the crown should suggest a horseshoe shape. Members of this breed are known for their friendly and affectionate natures.

Lop (Holland)

GROUPS: Agouti, Broken, Pointed White, Self, Shaded, Solid, Ticked

COLOR: All colors within the recognized groups

WEIGHT: Bucks and Does, not over 4 pounds

The Holland Lop is a solid and stocky little rabbit. In its general appearance, the animal is compact and balanced

Holland Lop. This compact, tiny rabbit is the smallest of the lop rabbit breeds.

throughout. Ideally, the ears are to hang closely to the cheeks. They should be in balance with the rest of the body and with the head. The

Mini Lop. This breed was developed in Germany, where it is known as the *Klein Widder* (Little Hanging Ear). This specimen has nice distinct markings.

Holland Lop is known for its lively and inquisitive personality.

Lop (Mini)

GROUPS: Agouti, Broken, Pointed White, Self, Shaded, Solid, Ticked

COLORS: All colors within the recognized groups

WEIGHT: Bucks and Does, 4 ½ to 6 ½ pounds

The Mini Lop is thickset and solid. Its

Mini Rex. A velvet-like coat is the outstanding feature of this breed.

broad shoulders have good depth and are well filled. Compactness and balance are reflected in the animal's overall appearance. Mini Lop does are known for their good parental instincts.

Mini Rex

VARIETIES: Blue, Californian, Castor, Chinchilla, Opal, Lynx, Red, Seal, Tortoise, White, Broken Group

WEIGHT: Bucks 3 to 4 ¼ pounds; Does 3 ¼ to 4 ½ pounds

In general appearance, the Mini Rex is diminutive, balanced, and uniform throughout. An ideal specimen of the breed will also be short in the body and well proportioned.

Netherland Dwarf

GROUPS: Self, Shaded, Agouti, Tan Pattern, Any Other Variety

COLORS: Selfs—White, Black, Blue, Chocolate, Lilac; Shaded—Siamese Sable, Siamese Smoke Pearl, Sable Point; Agouti—Chinchilla, Lynx, Opal, Squirrel, Chestnut; Tan Pattern—Sable Marten, Silver Marten, Smoke Pearl Marten, Otter, Tans; Any Other Variety—Fawn, Himalayan, Orange, Steel, Tortoiseshell.

WEIGHT: Bucks and Does, not over 2 ½ pounds

A trio of Netherland Dwarfs exhibiting but a few of the many colors that are available in this breed.

A white ruby-eyed Netherland Dwarf.

Some people have chosen to keep Netherland Dwarfs mainly because they want a small-sized rabbit. The housing needs for these rabbits are quite modest compared to the other rabbit breeds.

The Netherland Dwarf is the smallest of all the breeds of rabbit and has the greatest variety of colors and patterns. It is an imported breed from the Netherlands, and its popularity has grown steadily. Not since the days of importation of the Belgian Hare has any one breed so caught the attention of fancy.

The Netherland Dwarf has a short, compact, cobby body with wide shoulders. The coat is dense, and the ears are rather small in comparison to body size.

New Zealand

VARIETIES: Black,

A red New Zealand. This is a very solid, meaty breed.

Red, and White

WEIGHT: Bucks 9 to 11 pounds; Does 10 to 12 pounds

The New Zealand is considered to be the all-purpose rabbit—bred for meat, fur, show, and laboratory use. The appearance suggests good balance and uniformity, with the body well-fleshed. The body should be medium in length and have good depth and width, suggesting a solid animal.

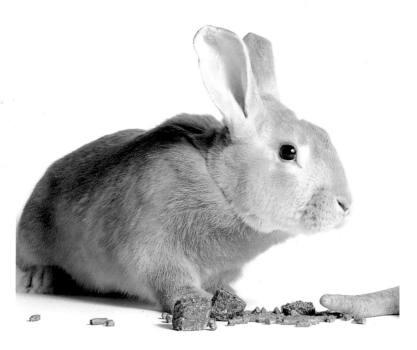

In a golden Palomino (shown here), the eyes are brown; in a lynx Palomino, they are blue-gray.

Palomino

VARIETIES: Golden and Lynx

WEIGHT: Bucks 8 to 10 pounds; Does 9 to 11 pounds

This is a breed developed in the United States to be equal to the New Zealand in quality and to be attractive in color. As in all utility rabbits, the Palomino

A male golden Palomino. This specimen is a pet-quality rabbit.

has a body that is well fleshed. The back has a gradual arch so as to appear rounded in the back, loin, and hindquarters.

The Golden variety is an attractive shade of gold with cream or white undercolor. The Lynx variety has a pearl-gray surface coloration that blends into the intermediate coloration of orange/ beige. The undercolor appears light cream to white.

Polish

VARIETIES: Black, Blue,

Chocolate, Blue-eyed White, Ruby-eyed White

WEIGHT: Bucks and Does, not over 3 ½ pounds

This is a popular exhibition rabbit. It is raised strictly for show, and fanciers have developed a Blue-Eyed White and a Ruby-Eyed White, which are shown as separate varieties.

The body is small and compact with well-rounded hips. The short

A Polish as seen in the United States. The Polish, which is a spritely little rabbit, has an overall appearance of roundness.

A Polish as seen in Great Britain. It is available in a number of colors. (In the United States, the counterpart to this breed is the Britannia Petite, which comes only in white.)

fur is fine and dense. It is fly-back and lies medium close to the body. The head is medium full, short, and has a slight curvature in the skull from ear to nose.

Rex. The Rex coat, which is short and stands upright from the body, is the result of a mutation.

Rex

VARIETIES: Black, Black Otter, Blue, Californian, Castor, Chinchilla, Chocolate, Lilac, Lynx, Opal, Red, Sable, Seal, White, Broken Group

WEIGHT: Bucks 7 ½ to 9 ½ pounds; Does 8 to 10 ½ pounds

This breed was developed from a mutation of the normal-coated rabbit. Unlike normal rabbit fur, with its longer guard hairs, the Rex coat has no conspicuous guard hairs; they are present but are of the same length as the undercoat. The breed is well proportioned with a medium-length body having good depth and well-rounded hips. It is filled out in the loins, typical of meat-type rabbits.

Rhinelander

COLOR: White with markings of black and bright golden-orange

WEIGHT: Bucks 6 ½ to 9 ½ pounds; Does 7 to 10 pounds

In general appearance, the Rhinelander's body is rounded and closely resembles a cylindrical

A red female Rex. The coloration of the ears is noticeably lighter than that of the body.

shape. The length of the animal should be such that it gives the appearance of grace. The Rhinelander projects an overall impression of attentiveness and vivacity.

Rhinelanders. This breed, which is quite popular in Europe, has a black and golden-orange coloration against a white background.

Satin. The hair shells of this breed are transparent, which causes them to reflect light. This quality is reflected in the sheen of the Satin's fur.

The well-shaped head, which is set closely on the shoulders, should be in balance with the body.

Satin

VARIETIES: Black, Blue, Californian, Chinchilla, Chocolate, Copper, Red, Siamese, White, and Broken Group

WEIGHT: Bucks 8 ½ to 10 ½ pounds; Does 9 to 11 pounds

Developed in the United States, the

A female Silver. This breed is one of those more frequently seen on the show circuit.

Satin is distinguishable by the beautiful sheen of its fur. The quality of the Satin's fur is the result of a mutation.

In overall appearance, the Satin is of medium length, with rather short legs. The Satin has its own standard by which its fur is judged.

Silver

VARIETIES: Black, Brown, Fawn

WEIGHT: Bucks and Does, 4 to 7 pounds

This is another of the fancy breeds, bred mainly for show. The body is plump with good

Silver Marten. Silver-tipped guard hairs create the unique appearance of this breed.

loins and firm flesh. It gives a handsome appearance. Color is of prime importance, with the top color as silvery as possible and ticked with white throughout the entire body, head, ears, and feet.

The colors of the Silver's undercolor are: a deep blue in the Black variety, chestnut-brown in the Brown variety, and a rich orange shade in the Fawn variety.

Silver Fox

VARIETIES: Blue, Black

WEIGHT: Bucks 9 to 11 pounds; Does 10 to 12 pounds

This is a large, meaty breed. The body is broad, meaty, and slightly arched. It has a deep loin and is medium in length with medium bone. The most unique feature about this rabbit is its long, silvery coat, which resembles fox fur.

Silver Marten

VARIETIES: Black, Blue, Chocolate, Sable

WEIGHT: Bucks 6 ½ to 8 ½ pounds; Does 7 ½ to 9 ½ pounds

This breed is a sport (mutation) from the Chinchilla. The unique appearance of the fur is due to silver-tipped guard hairs. In developing the Chinchilla breed, a black Tan was introduced. The Silver Marten is silver in those areas where the black Tan is tan. In England, this breed is known as the Silver Fox rabbit.

Tan

VARIETIES: Black, Blue, Chocolate, Lilac

WEIGHT: Bucks 4 to 5 ½ pounds; Does 4 to 6 pounds

It is believed that the original Black and Tan rabbits were sports from the

Opposite: A show-quality Tan. The hallmark of the Tan is its deep, rich tan coloration, which is primarily on the underside of the body.

mating between a wild rabbit and a Dutch. The markings of the Tan rabbit are a stable genetic feature. The body color is solid, free of white hairs. The tan markings should be rich and bright. They appear on the triangle that encircles the neck, the inner part of the front and hind legs, the chest, belly, flanks, eye circles, inside edges of the ears, and underside of the tail. The body of the Tan is compact and slightly arched.

A pair of black Tans. This breed also comes in three other color varieties: blue, chocolate, and lilac. The colors are enhanced by the shiny quality of the coat.

Housing and Maintenance

Climate, comfort, and sanitation are the primary factors to consider when planning housing for rabbits. The more thought and planning put into the housing of the rabbit that you will keep, the less work and expense there will be in the end. Many pet shops stock cages, as well as other kinds of

A Flemish Giant and a New Zealand. Cramped living quarters can cause stress, which can lower a rabbit's resistance to illness.

This portable outdoor enclosure can be moved to any desired location so that its occupant can graze at will. Its only drawback is that it is contructed of chicken wire, which is not durable and is subject to a rabbit's gnawing on it.

Art. # H-293

Art. # H-301

Your pet shop dealer can help you to select the right accommodations for your rabbit. Photo, courtesy of Rolf C. Hagen Corp.

supplies, that are specially designed for rabbits. Although metal cages may seem an unnecessary expense when compared to a wood hutch or a cardboard box, the rabbits will fare far better. Wood hutches are satisfactory, but in the long run they become unsanitary and are difficult to clean. There is no need to go into detail about the cardboard box. Once the bottom is urine soaked or the rabbit chews its way out, the box will end up in the trash heap.

If your ultimate goal is to raise a *large* number of rabbits, there are two ways to go about it. One is the colony method, in

If you choose to house your rabbit in an outdoor hutch, the top of it will have to be equipped with some type of weatherproof material.

which, space permitting, a colony consisting of one buck and several does is maintained on the ground in a fenced enclosure. The fence *must* extend two feet below the surface of the ground to prevent the rabbits from escaping. This is ideal where annual rainfall is minimal or in areas where good drainage is provided.

The arid climate of the southwestern states, where annual rainfall is frequently a mere three inches, lends itself well to colony raising. The does dig into the earth to give birth and are cool in summer and warm in winter. However, in locales

A Flemish Giant nibbling on hay. Your rabbit's accommodations should be located in a draft-free location.

Letting your rabbit loose on elevated surfaces is not a good idea: if he is suddenly startled or frightened, he may jump down and injure himself.

where heavy rainfall is normal, entire litters of newborn rabbits may drown during the first thunderstorm.

The second and most popular method of housing a number of rabbits is with well-designed metal hutches. They are long-lasting, sturdy, and easy to clean and maintain. They can also be equipped with water fountains and feeders that can be filled from outside the cage, saving time and labor.

No matter what type of cage that you choose, the floor should provide solid footing and at the same time allow waste material to fall through.

When utilizing two-tier cages, a piece of solid metal should be placed between the upper and lower cages. This metal partition can slope toward the back of the cage at such an angle as to drain urine from the upper cage to the ground, or it may be fashioned in such a manner as to act as a collector pan with raised sides. The urine from the upper cage is then caught and held to prevent contact with either the ground or the cage below. These pans should be cleaned at least twice a week.

The dimensions for hutches or cages vary with the size of the rabbit breed. A cage to house a breed of medium size is 18 inches high and 36 inches wide by 30 inches long. For the giant breeds, 36 inches by 60 inches or up to 72 inches by 24 inches is preferred, and small breeds need only 24

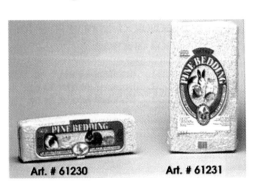

Art. # 61230   Art. # 61231

Absorbent and inexpensive bedding material can be purchased at your pet shop. Photo, courtesy of Rolf C. Hagen Corp.

inches by 24 inches by 18 inches high. Hutches may be constructed of wood and wire mesh. If made entirely of wire mesh, they may be set on wooden legs or suspended by wires from the ceiling of a building. Since the worst hazards to rabbits are cold winds and high temperatures, the cages should be protected from sun in summer and wind and rain in winter.

In mild climates, cages may be placed out of doors in a shaded area or provided with shade by means of an open-end building. In more severe climates, the rabbits should be housed indoors with

A Netherland Dwarf in his travel cage. This is the safest way to transport your rabbit for trips to the vet, vacations, and the like.

good ventilation. The addition of heat in winter is an asset. If no heat is available, lights may be suspended above the nest boxes to warm the young.

In the summer, heat prostration is the greatest threat to raising healthy rabbits. Not only do rabbits die if overheated or if allowed to remain in the sun without protection, but also the buck will become temporarily sterile when the temperature remains above 90° F for over 30 days.

When only a few rabbits are maintained, it is impractical to provide air-conditioned housing, but there are methods to keep the stock cool. One method

This rabbit has come to the front of his hutch to investigate what is being offered for dinner.

is to soak small blankets with cool water and place the blankets inside the cages for the rabbits to lie on. Another is to freeze gallon jugs of water and place a jug inside each cage. The rabbits will lie against the frozen jug, thereby cooling themselves. The jugs should be removed and replaced when thawed.

Even the beginner will want a feeder and a waterer that attaches to the outside of the hutch for ease of cleaning and filling. Modern methods of feeding and watering will give the rabbitry a neat appearance.

Water is the most critical element needed to keep rabbits from going off feed, and automatic watering

This simple-design hutch offers both an outdoor exercise pen and an enclosed area for sleeping.

Young Netherland Dwarfs, black and blue-eyed white. Rabbits enjoy variety in their diets.

systems afford fresh clean water on a continuous basis to each hutch. In severe weather where freezing is a problem, the pipes can be wrapped with heat cables, or cables can be inserted inside the pipes and thermostatically controlled.

Some breeders use crockery for water containers. Crockery is satisfactory as long as the temperature remains above freezing. When winter temperatures take a dive and the water in the crocks freezes, it is impossible to get the water to thaw without damage to the crocks. Frequently, the freezing alone will cause cracking and leakage.

An alternative to a crockery water container is a gravity-fed water botttle. Water bottles, which can be attached to the side of the cage, prevent rabbits from soiling their water supply.

Feeders should be attachable to the outside of the cage and have a mesh or screen bottom to allow dust from the pellets to filter out. Feed containers placed inside the cage invite the rabbits to sit in them, particularly the young near weaning age that are beginning to sample adult feed. The baby rabbits will soil the feed, making it unsanitary.

Nest boxes in a variety of designs are available for purchase. The average size is 8 inches high and 18 inches long by 12 inches wide. However, the size of the breed should be considered. There should always be room enough for the doe to turn around in the box but not enough excess room to encourage remaining in

Corn cobs are very absorbent and can be used to line the tray of your pet's cage. Photo, courtesy of Rolf C. Hagen Corp.

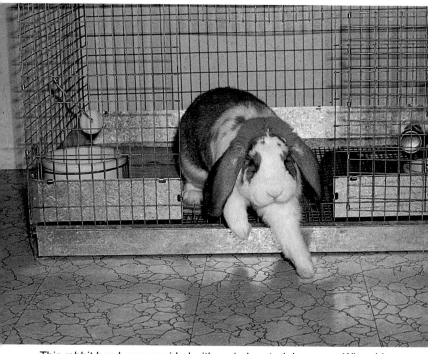

This rabbit has been provided with an indoor training cage. When his owner is home, he is allowed access to several rooms in the house.

the nest when her duties of caring for the young are complete. One side must be low enough to allow the doe to enter without damage to herself by striking the edge as she leaps in or out.

Regular cleaning of cages and nest boxes is essential for sanitation. After weaning each litter, the boxes are cleaned by washing with water and a disinfectant, scrubbing with a brush, then drying in the sun. They are then stored and ready for the next litter.

Rabbits select one corner of the cage to be used as a toilet, and although wire mesh is used, the droppings do not always fall through and will accumulate in this corner. Scraping the wire bottom or hosing it before it becomes heavily soiled will keep the cage clean. The build-up of hair can also pose a problem if not removed periodically. Most commercial rabbitries use a torch to burn it away, but a hose can be used satisfactorily. It is good practice to keep several empty cages on hand. The rabbits can then be rotated into these cages while their own quarters are being cleaned. If the rabbit keeper works frequently with his animals and handles them in a calm manner, they will be gentle and easy to care for; and the small problems that arise can be checked before they become large ones.

Opposite: Greenfoods are a supplement to a rabbit's diet. They should never be fed in large quantities.

Feeding and Nutrition

Feeding rabbits has never been more easy or more beneficial for the stock. Large feed companies have spent many years researching the dietary requirements of rabbits and developing pelleted feeds that are nutritionally balanced. Research has produced products that are not only high in nutrition but also consistently high in quality and palatability.

It is far easier, safer, and cheaper to feed commercially made products, which are

Contrary to popular notion, carrots are not a mainstay of a rabbit's diet. Rabbits do enjoy carrots, but they should be considered a treat.

Hard, dry bread will be much appreciated by your pet. It will give him the opportunity to gnaw, which helps to keep the teeth worn down.

Above *and* ***Below:*** *Pet shops stock all kinds of food items, including pellets and treats. Photos, courtesy of Rolf C. Hagen Corp.*

Art. # H-1163   Art. # H-1164

available at pet shops, than to try to understand the subject of nutrition and to meet the animal's dietary requirements. Improper feeding leads to disease, rickets, anemia, low fertility, and poor growth. On the other hand, with good feeding, good management, and disease control, rabbits can be maintained in fit condition for both production and show.

Supplements are not necessary, but good-quality legumes or grass hay may be occasionally added to the diet. Legumes include alfalfa, lespedeza, cowpea, vetch, peanut, and clover. Some rabbit hobbyists like to offer

Female American Fuzzy Lop. She is eating pelleted rabbit food and a hay cube.

their pets alfalfa hay cubes; others prefer to feed dried hay that is unprocessed.

Hay can be particularly beneficial when a rabbit goes off feed due to very warm weather. A little hay fed during this time will entice even the most sluggish eater to dine.

Rabbits enjoy grain. It is a very basic part of the diet and is added to most pelleted feeds. Grains that can be offered as an occasional treat include oats, wheat, barley, sorghum grain, buckwheat, rye, and soft varieties of corn. Other *occasional* treats enjoyed by rabbits are root crops such as beets, carrots, turnips, and fresh greens that are free of pesticides.

There are three methods of feeding rabbits, and each has its advantages.

Free-feeding is the practice of keeping feed in front of each

A gravity-fed water bottle and an assortment of dry food and greenfood.

There is a wide variety of nutritious treat foods from which you can select. Photo, courtesy of Rolf C. Hagen Corp.

rabbit at all times. It is used mainly when growing young to market size, when conditioning an animal for show, or when feeding pregnant or lactating does. Each of these circumstances is considered a condition of stress.

Jersey Wooly. In essence, this breed is a dwarf angora-type rabbit.

Mini Lop and friend. Many rabbits enjoy the warmth and security of human contact.

Limit-feeding is feeding a limited amount to a rabbit. This method is used to prevent over-consumption of feed, which leads to weight problems. An overweight rabbit is less likely to reproduce. Bucks that are not in service and dry does are fed by this method. It is also used after weaning a litter to aid the doe in stopping the flow of milk.

Hand-feeding is daily feeding of the amount the rabbit would consume if feed were kept before it at all times. Enough feed must be given to maintain a steady rate of growth in young animals and to keep mature animals in top condition without excess fat. This is a preferred method in most rabbitries when it is combined with limit-feeding. It is ideal for does in production and for growing young.

The most important element in feeding is *water*. No animal can survive without it. Several factors affect the amount of water that a rabbit will consume. One of them is the temperature of the environment.

Mealtime for this group of Dutch rabbits. Note the sturdy crock bowls, which are untippable.

from the body, aids in digesting food, and functions in moving nutrients to and from the cells of the body tissues. It constitutes up to 75 percent of the adult animal body and as much as 95 percent

This Dwarf Hotot exhibits every visible aspect of good health.

Your rabbit's diet can be supplemented with hay, which is a source of fiber. Photo, courtesy Rolf C. Hagen Corp.

Rabbits are heat-sensitive animals and will consume great quantities of water during warm weather. This water disperses heat and helps adjust body temperature. Water also helps to remove impurities

Mini Rex, male and female. Like many other pets, rabbits can become overweight if they are fed too much.

of the weight of the newborn. A ten-pound rabbit will drink about ⅔ of a quart of water per day. This amount may increase with lactation or with warm weather. Because of the importance water plays in nutrition and health, it must be kept before the rabbit at all times.

Salt is another important element in feeding. However, pelleted feed contains necessary salt along with the other important minerals. Adding salt in the form of a salt spool is common, and the rabbit probably enjoys

than does reproduction. Because of this, no other natural function is of greater stress than nursing the young. The doe that is fed poorly is unable to maintain her body weight and produce milk at the same time. When the milk is insufficient for the litter, the young do not grow and develop properly. It is doubtful that undernourished young ever meet their full potential, so the doe must have sufficient protein to raise a healthy litter.

A little-known fact is that rabbits re-ingest their food, a practice known as coprophagy. It is normal for the rabbit to re-ingest a soft matter passed through the digestive tract. Rabbits excrete two kinds of feces, one hard and one soft. The ingestion of the soft kind provides a source of *B vitamins.* These vitamins are synthesized in the caecum by bacteria that are present. The caecum, a part of the intestine, normally synthesizes all the B vitamins that the rabbit requires.

Vitamin A is necessary to both animals and man. It is beneficial in combating stress and for healthy skin. Vitamin A is also known as the vitamin most needed for good eyesight and can be found in its natural state in all yellow

Wash all greenfoods thoroughly before feeding them to your rabbit.

vegetables. Persons with a vitamin A deficiency suffer from night blindness. Since rabbits are nocturnal, their eyesight is highly developed; perhaps this is why rabbits have always been associated with eating carrots, a good source of vitamin A. However, there is no real need to add carrots to a rabbit's diet, as most manufactured feed contains ample amounts of vitamin A in the form of vitamin A palmitate.

Vitamin D prevents rickets, as it aids in the assimilation of calcium by the body. It is required by rabbits in moderate amounts and is added to most pelleted feed.

Vitamin E deficiency in rabbits will cause degeneration of the skeletal muscles. It

A well-balanced diet will help to ensure the good health of this youngster now and throughout its adult life.

Young Mini Rex rabbits flanked by their parents.

will also cause infertility in the doe. In commercially manufactured feed, vitamin E is added in the form of alpha-tocopherol.

Vitamin K is important for the coagulation of blood, and research has proven a link between vitamin K and healthy bones. Scientists at the University of North Carolina at Chapel Hill discovered that a diet deficient in vitamin K, when fed to baby chicks for only five days, caused a ten-percent reduction in the mineral content of their bones. This vitamin is added in adequate amounts to manufactured feed.

A rabbit has the ability to make all the *vitamin C* that its body requires under normal conditions. Because of this, vitamin C is not added to manufactured feed.

Crude fat is necessary to provide energy. It is high in calories and is added to commercial feed at the rate of two to three percent. It decreases the dustiness of pelleted feed and adds palatability. Too high of a percentage of added fat will add fat to the rabbit in the form of increased body weight.

Fiber is necessary for the healthy movement of digested materials through the intestinal tract. A percentage of it is digested by the microflora present in the caecum. Since it adds bulk to the diet and is largely undigestible, it is understandable that feed high in fiber is lower in food value per unit of weight than is feed that is low in fiber. The major crude fiber added to commercial pellets comes from alfalfa hay.

Feeding rabbits need not be expensive or time consuming. Commercially manufactured feed meets all the dietary requirements of rabbits and takes the guesswork out of maintaining a well-nourished rabbit.

Close-up of a Netherland Dwarf. Rabbits have keen senses of smell and hearing.

Illness and Disease

This chapter in no way is meant to replace a qualified veterinarian, but rather it is to assist the rabbit owner in recognizing illness in his rabbits and treating it before it becomes epidemic in size. It is advisable to become acquainted with a qualified veterinarian on whom you can rely if problems arise. Many diseases are easily diagnosed and treated

A rabbit has 28 teeth, including four upper and two lower incisors. The main pair of upper incisors are in the front; the second, smaller pair lies behind the main pair.

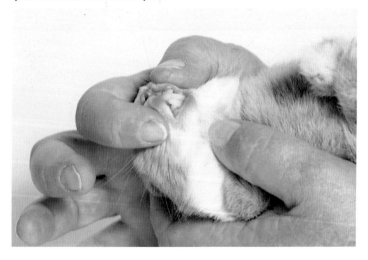

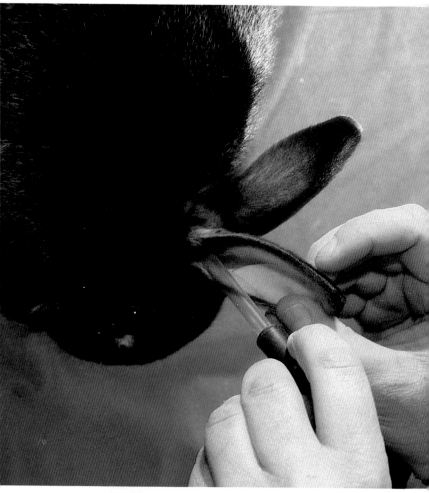

Rabbits can be subject to ear infestation by mites, signs of which will be evidenced by a crusty matter. Medications are available that contain insecticides and fungistats.

in the hutch, yet there are many that require the experience of a veterinarian or a veteran rabbit raiser.

The best remedy for disease is prevention. This is achieved by sanitation and good management. Another important step toward maintaining healthy rabbits is isolation.

This is not to imply that rabbits are to be kept in isolated quarters, but that visitors should be kept to a minimum. People can carry disease from one rabbitry to another, so it is best to avoid showing stock to strangers who may have spent the day visiting various

Chinchilla Mini Rex. Pelleted rabbit food eliminates the need for a rabbit owner to formulate a special diet for his pet.

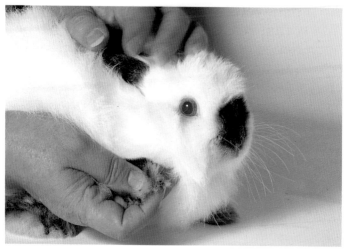

Jersey Wooly. A rabbit's nails can become overly long and may get caught on a wire floor. Check your rabbit's nails regularly and have them trimmed if they are too long.

rabbitries or who may have sick rabbits at home.

Stray dogs, cats, and wild animals such as mice, rats, and wild rabbits are carriers of disease and contaminants. Feed should be stored in such a manner as to prevent the invasion of mice. Never introduce a new rabbit to your stock without knowing from where it has come.

Infectious agents that cause disease in rabbits are bacteria, viruses, parasites, and fungi. They are the same agents that cause illness in other animals

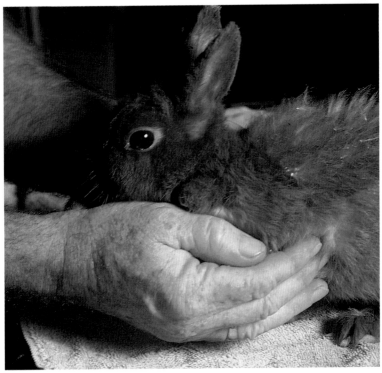

This Netherland Dwarf is suffering from skin mange, which should be treated with a powder specially formulated for external parasites. Check with your vet.

and in man. Although direct contact is necessary in some instances, this is not always the case, as viruses and fungi are carried in the air. This explains how an outbreak of a virus can spread so rapidly.

This unfortunate rabbit has an advanced case of snuffles. Note the wet front paws, which it has used to wipe the discharge from its nose. Compounding the problem is an eye infection known as conjunctivitis.

ABSCESSES

Symptoms: Lumps under the skin in the back, neck, cheek, or dewlap areas.

Cause: Abscesses are a collection of pus caused by the invasion of a bacterium, *streptococcus*.

Treatment: Abscesses must be drained of

infective matter—a procedure that should be performed by a veterinarian. After an abscess is drained, it is essential that it be kept clean. Additionally, your vet may also suggest the application of an antibiotic ointment or an antimicrobic spray or powder.

CANNIBALISM

Symptoms: Scattered remnants of flesh in the nestbox or missing young from the nest box within two weeks after kindling.

Cause: Does with first litters are easily excitable and are under stress. They may eat their young if disturbed

Netherland Dwarfs: blue, blue-eyed white, and chocolate.

Experienced rabbit keepers clip their own rabbits' nails, but the novice rabbit owner should have the procedure performed by a vet.

suddenly, such as by a strange dog. However, it has been the author's experience that cannibalism can occur even when no disturbance has taken place. There seem to be two factors involved. The first is diet, and the second is heredity. It may also be a means by which the doe reduces the number of young to that which she can satisfactorily nurse.

Treatment: First decide the cause. If the doe was frightened and became cannibalistic, prevent any further disturbance. Be careful to prevent stess-inducing situations (e.g., loud noises) or move her cage to a secluded spot before the arrival of future litters.

If diet is the cause, a protein supplement added to the diet a few days before kindling will give a protein boost and will aid in the production of milk.

When the litter is too large, moving some of the young to a doe that has a small litter can be effective.

Never save young does for future breeding stock from the litter of a doe who shows signs of cannibalism, as this tendency may be passed on to the young.

CAKED UDDER

Symptoms: Does that are heavy milk producers are the most commonly affected, particularly when nursing only a few young. The teats become sore and the udder inflamed. The udder is hard and hot

Opposite: One of the primary symptoms of skin mange is loss of hair.

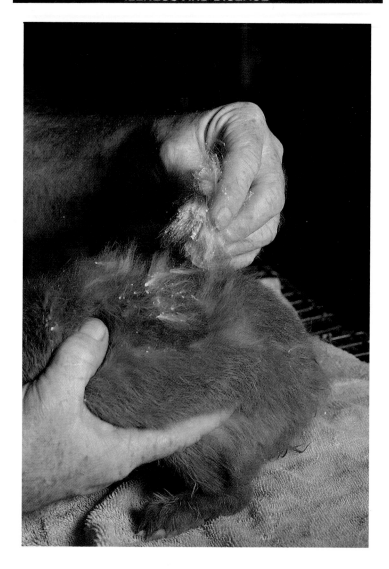

Himalayan. A healthy rabbit will be alert and interested in its surroundings.

to the touch. The doe may refuse to nurse the litter.

Cause: The most frequent cause is too few young to relieve the flow of milk. A doe will easily bruise herself when leaping in or out of the nest box if the sides of the box are too high. Another cause is improper weaning.

Treatment: For mild cases, such as

improper weaning, whereby the young were removed suddenly before milk production slowed, cut back on feed and return one or two of the litter for a day or two. Where too few young are being nursed, add one or more young from a doe with a large litter.

In the event that the teats are injured, sore, or cracked, apply an antibiotic ointment, which will not only aid in healing but will also soften the skin to prevent further cracking. This condition is frequently seen in does with their first litters.

Do not fail to treat a caked udder as soon as it is detected. If

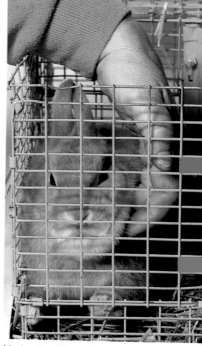

Netherland Dwarf. All cages, including carrying cages, should be cleaned regularly to prevent the accumulation of harmful bacteria.

untreated, it can lead to the destruction of the udder, leaving it non-functional.

A fawn Netherland Dwarf.

SORE HOCKS

Symptoms: Sitting in a hunched position. Inactivity and off feed. The presence of scabs or sores on front or hindleg hocks. Infection may cause swelling and inflammation.

Cause: This is a painful condition that is caused mainly by unsanitary conditions in the cage, sharp wire flooring, or cage bottoms that are not solid enough to support the rabbit's weight without sagging. Some rabbits inherit thin fur covering on the feet and are more susceptible.

Treatment: Wash the sores with mild soap and water. Apply an antibiotic ointment until the condition clears. Placing a board on the cage floor will give relief until healing is complete. If the animal shows no signs of improvement, check with a veterinarian.

FUNGUS INFECTION

Symptoms: Hairless patches of skin with a flaky, dry crust. The lesions appear on the nose, feet, around the mouth, on the eyelids, and on the backs of the ears.

Cause: A fungus invasion of the hair follicles. Fungus is transmitted by people handling the stock or spread from one rabbit to another on contact.

French Lop. A rabbit's fur should be free of any bare or irritated patches of skin.

This condition is also transmissible to man, so caution should be used when handling affected animals.

Treatment: Rub a fungus powder or ointment into affected area daily until new hair growth appears. Replace bedding in nest boxes and apply fungus powder to the fresh bedding to prevent transmission of fungus to the young.

MUCOID ENTERITIS

Symptoms: Diarrhea as evidenced by feces on the hind feet or not forming into the usual round pill shape; hunched back, rough coat, grinding the teeth, or sitting hunched over the water dish with front feet in the water. The stomach may be bloated, and the eyes appear to be squinting.

Cause: Fifty percent of all rabbit deaths from birth to eight weeks of age are caused by mucoid enteritis. The exact cause is not known, but it is suspected to be caused by one or more of the following: coccidiosis, intestinal parasites, fungi, virus, unsanitary conditions and/or improper feeding.

Treatment: A water-soluble antibiotic can be added to the drinking water at the rate of one teaspoon per 2 ½ gallons of water. Continue

Opposite: Bright eyed, alert, and well furred, this Dutch rabbit appears to be the picture of good health.

treatment for one week. As a preventive measure, the stock may be treated with a low-level mixture at the rate of one teaspoon per five gallons of water.

Anticoccidials or sulfa solutions, which are primarily used by poultry breeders, prove to be highly beneficial when coccidiosis is the cause. The amount recommended for poultry is printed on the label of the bottle and is satisfactory for rabbits. Mix this solution with the drinking water and

English Spot. The nose marking on this rabbit is evenly balanced.

A young male Netherland Dwarf.

offer as the only water available to sick animals, or use it periodically to treat the stock as a preventive measure. Do not administer two drugs at the same time.

Mucoid enteritis is a deadly disease. Animals that die from mucoid enteritis must be disposed of in a manner that is in accordance with local health regulations.

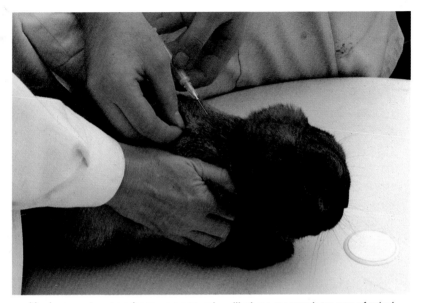

Having a vet upon whom you can rely will give you much peace of mind should your rabbit become ill.

COCCIDIOSIS

Symptoms: A listless appearance, pot belly, loss of appetite, thinness, and diarrhea. Upon examination, the liver will be spotted white and the intestine inflamed. A heavy mucous will be found in the intestines.

Cause: Coccidia are microscopic parasites that grow in the intestines. They are transmitted via drinking contaminated water or by the normal eating of the offal.

Treatment: The use of sulfa solutions on a regular monthly basis is a control measure. For acute cases, use the solution for three days, then withhold for three days, then give for a final three days. Follow instructions printed on the label as given for poultry.

PNEUMONIA

Symptoms: Rapid breathing, a temperature above 103° F, nasal discharge, and a bluish tint to the eye color of albinos.

Cause: Drafty, cold, or damp quarters. Stress and a general run-down condition weaken the rabbit's

A pair of Steel Dutch rabbits.

ability to fight off bacterial infections. The infection invades the lungs and nasal passages. It is a major killer of adult

A gravity-fed bottle will help to prevent contamination of your rabbit's drinking water. Photo, courtesy Rolf C. Hagen Corp.

rabbits and can infect and kill a rabbit within 24 hours. Suspect pneumonia when one occupant of a rabbitry is discovered dead without any previous sign of illness.

Treatment: Speed in diagnosing and treating this disease is of the utmost importance. Veterinary treatment will likely include injection of antibiotics.

CONJUNCTIVITIS

Symptoms: This is an inflammation of the eye that is manifested by tearing or a discharge of pus. In severe cases, the eye may be stuck closed.

There are a number of medications available for the treatment of minor cuts and bruises.

Cause: Bacteria that have infected the eye, or irritants such as dust, pollen, or foreign objects.

Treatment: Cleanse the eye with a mild solution of boric acid or sterile water. Apply an antibiotic eye ointment once or twice daily until the condition clears.

EAR CANKER

Symptoms: Shaking of the head and scratching at the ear. The formation of crust deep within the ear.

Cause: Ear mites, which embed themselves into the soft parts of the ear.

Treatment: The

mites that cause ear canker will spread quickly from one rabbit to another. Isolate infected animals. Apply a drop or two of mineral oil to suffocate the offending mites and repeat the treatment in 10 to 14 days. Effective remedies are available that contain insecticides and fungistats. Check with your vet.

MASTITIS

Symptoms: Tender, sore, or swollen milk glands with bluish coloring. Severe cases may be abscessed.

Cause: An injury to the milk glands. The doe may have bruised herself when jumping into the nest box, or damaged herself on sharp objects such as nails, wires, or rough edges of the nest box. Mastitis is also

Rabbit hutches of an older design. The chicken-wire fronts are not a good idea, as the rabbits can gnaw their way through them.

A nutritious mixture of rabbit pellets and other assorted dry foods.

caused by bacteria entering the rabbit's system, and young from an infected doe should not be placed in the nest box of an uninfected doe.

Treatment: Sanitize the nest box and hutch after each litter. Remove any sharp objects within the hutch, and ensure that each nest box has one side considerably lower than the other three. Check with your veterinarian, who will prescribe a course of treatment.

SNUFFLES

Symptoms: Snuffles is called, by many breeders, the common cold in rabbits because of the nasal discharge. There may be sneezing prior to the runny nose, and the affected rabbit tries to wipe away the discharge with his front paws.

Cause: An infection developing in the mucous membranes of the nasal passages due to stress and lowered resistance.

Treatment: Treat all of the stock by administering a water-soluble antibiotic in the

drinking water. Follow the manufacturer's directions on the package (usually one

This rabbit has a case of sarcoptic mange, which is caused by a mite. Many animals are subject to this condition, including dogs and cats.

An assortment of edible wild plants: dandelion, plaintain, and mallow.

teaspoon to every five gallons of water). Do not use metal water containers while using this medication.

This condition can also be treated by means of antibiotic injections. Consult your vet regarding such treatment. Do not use two medications at the same time.

STRESS
Symptoms: All growing and breeding

This is a safe way to lift a rabbit. With one hand, secure the fold of skin over the shoulders; with the other hand, grasp and lift the hindquarters. Under no circumstances should a rabbit ever be lifted by its ears.

This rabbit has an advanced case of coccidiosis. Symptoms of this illness, which is not uncommon in rabbits, include rough fur, thinness, loss of appetite, and diarrhea.

animals are under stress. Also, stress is seen in animals that are hauled to and from shows or otherwise moved from their normal quarters. Extremes of temperature, poor diet, parasites, illness, and strange visitors are other causes of stress. There may be diarrhea, unthriftiness, loss of weight, and in the case of pregnant does, aborted litters.

Causes: Any situation that puts a strain on the emotional or physical condition of the animal.

Treatment: Use a vitamin mixed with the water and feed a highly nutritious diet. Avoid

Netherland Dwarf. This is the smallest of all of the breeds of rabbit.

drafty quarters or overheated quarters, which may cause bucks to go sterile. Treat disease and parasites as quickly as they become recognized.

SLOBBERS

Symptoms: The rabbit will be wet about the face or throat, and the face may be swollen.

Cause: The feeding of fresh greens in excessive amounts when the digestive system is not accustomed to them. A sudden change in diet from pellets to greens is harsh on the animal's system; any change should be made gradually.

An abscessed or overgrown molar tooth may also be the cause.

Treatment: Discontinue the fresh greens until the condition clears itself. When the rabbit is cured, do not overfeed it with green foods. If an abscessed or overgrown tooth is the cause involved, it can be removed by your veterinarian.

TAPEWORM LARVAE

Symptoms: There are no symptoms of tapeworm larvae in a live rabbit. Examination of the liver tissue will disclose white streaks, or there may be small white cysts attached to the membranes of the stomach or the intestines.

Treatment: No treatment is available. Prevention is the only method of control. As tapeworm larvae are brought into the rabbitry by dogs and

This Jersey Wooly is having its teeth checked. It shows no evidence of malocclusion, which is a misalignment of the teeth.

This rabbit has ringworm. This disease is not common to rabbits and is usually the result of poor husbandry.

cats, these animals should never be allowed access to your rabbit's feed and water bowls or nest material.

KETOSIS

Symptoms: The rabbit refuses to eat, usually after kindling and following a normal pregnancy.

Cause: This is a metabolic disorder that releases ketone bodies into the rabbit's blood stream. The presence of ketones prevents hunger and produces the normal action of the body to absorb body fat. This in turn causes weight loss and eventual death.

Treatment: A change of diet is effective. Changing from pellets to alfalfa hay and grain will stimulate an interest in food. Also, adding sugar or molasses to the drinking water will get sugar into the bloodstream rapidly and stop the manufacture of ketones. Generally, does that are heavy producers of milk are more affected by ketosis.

English Lop. Lop rabbits require extra attention to their ears to prevent parasitic infestation and infection.

VENT DISEASE

Symptoms: The appearance of blisters or scabs on the genitals. Swollen genitals.

Cause: Vent disease is highly contagious and is frequently referred to among rabbit raisers as rabbit syphilis. If left untreated, the rabbit will become a dormant carrier of the disease (without showing any outward symptoms). It can then be transmitted to unborn young. The disease is caused by a bacterium.

It is possible to confuse vent disease with fungal or urine infection caused by unsanitary bedding. For proper diagnosis, consult your veterinarian and have laboratory tests run.

Treatment: Wash the genital area with warm water and a mild soap. Apply an antibiotic ointment daily until the condition improves. Where solid floors are used, the straw or other litter material should be changed daily.

Your veterinarian can prescribe a course of treatment.

ORCHITIS

Symptoms: Inflammation of the testicles.

Cause: A bacterium that is transmitted from one rabbit to another during mating. Unclean cages and hutch floors.

Treatment: It is best

Poisonous plants: poison hemlock, jimsonweed, and water hemlock. If you are interested in including wild plants in your pet's diet, you should first invest in a good wild-plant identification book.

to cull the affected buck rather than to attempt treatment with antibiotics.

METRITIS

Symptoms: A white, thick, putrid discharge exuded by does seven to ten days after breeding has taken place. This infection can invade the uterus and cause sterility in the doe.

Treatment: This infection is difficult to treat, and it is recommended that affected does be culled, as they may cause bucks to develop orchitis.

MALOCCLUSION OR BUCK TEETH

Symptoms: Loss of weight. Possible drooling and wetness about the mouth. Lower teeth that curve upward into the mouth, and upper teeth that curve inward into the mouth.

Cause: This is a hereditary condition in which the upper or lower jaw is too long or too short. Rabbits *must* be able to gnaw on objects to keep their teeth worn down. If their teeth do not meet properly, the proper gnawing action to wear them down is lacking, and the teeth continue to grow. Death will result unless treatment is available.

Treatment: Using a pair of sharp wire

Opposite: A white New Zealand and two Dutch, blue and black.

nippers, temporary relief can be given by clipping the incisors. If you are at all uncertain about how to perform this procedure, consult your veterinarian. This will give relief and enable the rabbit to eat.

However, since the condition is hereditary, the animal should not be used for breeding. With proper selection of breeding stock, this condition is easily eliminated in future generations.

Rabbits eating from a community feeder. Opponents of this kind of feeding method maintain that it can more easily lead to the spread of disease.

SPLAY LEG

Symptoms: Young rabbits that have difficulty in standing. The legs spread away from the body, and the animal sprawls on its belly. The very young rabbit will eat satisfactorily, but as it grows and gains weight, moving about becomes more difficult. Once weaning occurs (when the doe does not enter the nest box to nurse the litter), splay leg causes the growing youngster to have difficulty in reaching the feed. Soon it gives up and dies.

Cause: This is another hereditary condition that can be eliminated through

Overconsumption of greenfoods can lead to intestinal problems such as diarrhea.

careful selection of breeding stock. The bones and muscles of young rabbits prone to this condition never develop strength, and

New Zealand. Some believe that this breed is the result of a cross between a Flemish Giant mutation and a Belgian Hare.

there may even be some malformation of the hip joint.

Treatment: Young rabbits that show signs of having splay leg should be euthanised.

HEAT PROSTRATION

Symptoms: Rapid breathing, prostration, and, in severe cases, blood-tinged fluid emerging from the nostrils and mouth.

Cause: Does that are due to kindle and overweight older rabbits are most susceptible to extreme outside temperatures. Rabbits are heat-sensitive animals.

Treatment: Reduce the temperature of surrounding air by spraying with water. Place wet blankets or frozen jugs of water inside the cages for the rabbits to lie on or be near to reduce body temperature.

MYXOMATOSIS
Symptoms:
Inflammation and swelling of the eyes, ears, nose, and genitals. This illness is accompanied by a high fever. The death rate among mature animals is high.

Cause: This is a viral infection affecting rabbits only along the West Coast of the United States, Mexico, and South America. It is spread by biting insects

A red male New Zealand. This photo clearly indicates the meaty quality of the breed.

such as mosquitoes.

Treatment: The best control is prevention, since there is no cure. Spray or drain mosquito-breeding sites. There is a vaccine proven to be effective in the prevention of myxomatosis.

WARBLES

Symptoms: Irritated, raised areas under the skin, usually on the back, neck, or flanks. Movement can be felt under the skin. A visible hole can be seen on the skin's surface.

Cause: Botfly larvae, which enter under the skin and feed upon tissue. They obtain oxygen from the hole in the skin and must frequently surface to breathe.

Treatment: A drop of chloroform or ether on the larvae will quiet them for easy removal with a pair of tweezers or forceps. The larvae may be as much as 1 ½ inches in length. After removal, apply a skin antiseptic to the wound.

SKIN MANGE

Symptoms: Intense itching, red, scaly skin, loss of hair. A crust of yellow, dried blood serum may be present.

Cause: A microscopic mite that burrows under the skin.

Treatment: Dust with a powder especially formulated for external parasites such as fleas. Use two dustings, one week apart.

All of the plants shown above are non-edible: horsetail and hedge nettles (two varieties).

Breeding Better Rabbits

Breeding rabbits either as a hobby or as a profession is educational, fascinating, and enjoyable. And when several rabbit breeders come together with an interest in showing, it becomes competitive. Even in competition, there are no losers, as

A Rex doe and her baby. The fur of this breed is at its best when the animal reaches maturity.

This doe is making a nest for her young. The nest is made of soft fur that the doe has pulled from her belly.

Netherland Dwarfs. It is not always easy to gauge the quality of a young rabbit. In some cases, an accurate assessment cannot be made until the animal is closer to maturity.

everyone involved learns, improves, and enjoys. This is the reason competition among rabbit breeders has stood the test of time. The rabbit is the real winner: the animal has been improved upon in its usefulness and its beauty.

Since rabbits reproduce so rapidly and many generations of them can be produced in a lifetime of man, they are excellent subjects for studying the results of different breeding programs. Every characteristic, from color of fur to color of eye, from size to carriage of ear, is controlled by genes,

A black Dutch. The white markings on the hind feet are known as the *stops*. They should be clean cut and equal in length.

minute units of coded information that are passed on from one individual to another through inheritance.

I doubt that an animal breeder exists who does not want to improve his line. Even when starting with the best stock money can buy, there is something

Baby rabbits are adorable. This youngster's Dutch rabbits are just a few weeks old.

future generations. The only way to do this is to have a basic understanding of how genetics, the biology of heredity, works.

Taking the subject in its simplest form, genetics is simply the coming together of genes. Genes can be either dominant or recessive: A gene that masks the characteristic of another gene is said to be dominant; the gene that is masked is termed recessive. The dominant genes will show themselves in the young, while the recessive ones will be carried and may or may not show themselves. Only when two recessives come together will the

about breeding that makes a person strive for improvement in

A black Netherland Dwarf.

recessive trait make itself known. Such is the case of buck teeth or splay legs. If an individual in a litter of otherwise healthy and normal baby rabbits has either of these traits, it has inherited a recessive gene for the condition from each parent. The rest of the litter may be carrying this recessive gene to pass on to their young, or they may be clear.

When starting a breeding program, set up a plan to mate those individuals possessing

A doe nursing her young. Does can vary in their mothering capabilities.

Mini Lop. You must carefully evaluate the rabbits that you select for a breeding pair. The ones that you choose should be healthy and sound.

the desired traits for reaching an established goal. Such a goal may be to improve head, bone, or fur. It may be to increase or decrease size, or to maintain balance while increasing meatiness. Whatever the goal, remember that an end effect cannot be obtained unless the desired genes are present, even though they may be hidden. In other words, it is impossible to produce something that is not there, either in the parent stock or in the ancestors. There are only three types of breeding programs: *inbreeding*, *linebreeding*, and *outcrossing*.

Inbreeding is the mating of closely related animals. This can be the mating of littermate to littermate, father to daughter, or mother to son. It is the quickest method for setting a type, as the young will possess a uniform likeness and similar genetic makeup. With inbreeding, both desirable and undesirable traits can be passed on to future generations. The use of inbreeding will quickly reveal if certain animals are worthy of breeding at all. If the majority of the young are good, they are worth reproducing. If the majority are only fair or poor, it is better not to inbreed.

Linebreeding is the mating of closely related animals to maintain a high relationship to a particular ancestor. By selecting a highly desirable ancestor and breeding-related individuals that possess the same desirable traits, the young will carry many of the genes of that ancestor. Examples of linebreeding are the mating of nephew to

Opposite: A pet-quality rabbit, five weeks old.

Mini Lop. Breeding closely related animals is the quickest way to establish *type,* which is defined as the qualities that distinguish a breed.

aunt, cousin to cousin, and uncle to niece. Once a breeding program has been established and a goal maintained, this is the ultimate course to follow for continued success.

Outcrossing is the mating of unrelated individuals.

Outcrossing is unpredictable, as one never knows which recessive, or hidden, genes are carried. As many faults as good qualities can be introduced into stock by this method. Outcrossing is used when first starting out or when one has inbred or linebred until it is desirable to bring in new genes. Even then, it is more predictable to bring in a distant relative from another line.

SELECTING A PAIR

Neither the doe nor the buck has a greater hereditary influence on the offspring. However, since the buck is capable of servicing many does (and thereby capable of producing many more offspring than the doe), great care should be taken to procure the finest buck possible.

By following a few rules of thumb, a breeder can improve anything he wishes to

Mini Lop, broken pattern.

improve upon, whether it be longevity, good mothers, quiet disposition, or a number of physical characteristics. Select a male that has the ability to pass on his good points and those of his parents. That is to say, if it is desirable to improve milk production in your does, look for a male with a mother that is a good milk producer. When a male passes on his good qualities to his offspring, he is known to be what is termed *prepotent*. Not all outstanding individuals are capable of stamping their good points onto their young; and in such instances, little can be done to improve the quality of stock.

It is better to select a buck that comes from the stock of linebred individuals and is capable of passing the stock's finer points on to his young than to select a really fine specimen that has been the result of random breeding. Such a male is unlikely to produce young bearing his qualities.

Since, from the moment of fertilization, certain external conditions affect the well-being and development of the offspring, it is of the utmost importance to secure a sound, healthy doe and to give her a well-balanced, nutritious diet, sanitary housing, and a stress-free environment to produce many healthy litters.

Dwarf Hotot. The rabbits that you select for breeding should be in top physical condition—neither too fat nor too thin.

During the weeks of pregnancy, a host of factors can cause the death of embryos or a weakened condition of the young so that they die shortly after birth. Nature employs the

This youngster is enjoying the companionship of her pet rabbits, a Netherland Dwarf (adult) and a young mixed-breed rabbit.

means of aborting or resorbing the young to sustain the mother when an infection is present, or when the number of internal parasites is high. It is therefore important to keep the doe in top condition.

When external conditions affect the development of the young, they cannot be compensated for later. Even when inheritance has provided the genes for the making of exceptional individuals, improper diet can turn what would be straight, sound bones into undersized, crippled ones so that the young never attain normal size.

The same care used in selecting the buck should be used in selecting the doe. She should be as good a specimen of her breed as the buck, for even though environmental factors influence the development of the

A young male Rex.

young, they cannot make up for lack of soundness or good genetic makeup.

When the pair has produced a litter,

select the finer animals and breed them back to the parent stock. This will set the type, so that the next generation will be prepotent and able to pass on the good qualities they possess to their young. By following this method, a breeder can develop a line of rabbits unique to his rabbitry—animals that can become known for a particular quality that they possess and can pass on to offspring. The bucks will be sought after for breeding purposes,

A Siamese smoke pearl Netherland Dwarf.

A show-quality Satin Angora. If you are interested in breeding show rabbits, you should have a working knowledge of the standard for your chosen breed.

and the breeder can demand a high price for young stock once they prove themselves in the show ring.

Remember, too, that such close breeding will also set any bad characteristics carried by the parent stock, and these characteristics can be impossible to breed out. So the first pair must be selected with great care.

After the development of the desired characteristic in the stock, the plan of breeding should be changed to linebreeding, as previously discussed. A good example of this method would be to mate individuals that have a common ancestor such as the same grandparent or great-grandparent but whose other ancestors differ. By breeding these two individuals to each other, the young will possess double the number of genes for that grandparent or great-grandparent than would ordinarily be possible. Each baby rabbit inherits half of its genes from the buck and half from the doe; these genes, half from each parent, come together at the time of fertilization to produce the inheritance.

The influence of the grandparents on any specific characteristic diminishes 50 percent with each successive generation. By selecting a pair with the same ancestor, the amount of gene makeup contributed by that ancestor is increased. After familiarizing himself with the background of the stock and the grandparents, the breeder can select the ancestors with the same care used when purchasing the first breeding pair and produce young with a controlled heredity—maintaining good quality each successive generation, rather than losing it.

A black Tan. Selective breeding is a must if you are to achieve your desired breeding program goals.

Coat/Color Genetics

By Glenna M. Huffmon

In addition to the pleasures and satisfaction of raising a litter of rabbits, another of the main elements that draws rabbit fanciers into the breeding side of the hobby is the challenge of breeding for perfect color and perfect coat. A number of the beautiful colors and color patterns that we see in rabbits are the result of years of selective breeding efforts by conscientious, dedicated breeders.

RABBIT COAT COLORS

There is a vast array of coat colors found among the various breeds of rabbit. One of the most well known, of course, is the red-eyed rabbit with white coloration, which is seen in many of the breeds. This coloration is indicative of true albinism. There is no pigment anywhere on the rabbit.

There are also the Blue-Eyed Whites, which are found in breeds such as the Netherland Dwarf. The white coloration is pure white overall. There is no other color anywhere on the rabbit, except for the blue eyes. This type of coloration is sometimes called Vienna White.

Another kind of white-rabbit coloration is the Pointed White, or Himalayan, in which the main body is pure white but color is left on the *points*, which refer to the nose, ears, feet, and tail. This coloration is found on the Himalayan, the

A New Zealand. This rabbit is an albino, as evidenced by the red eyes and white coat.

Netherland Dwarf, the Jersey Wooly, and the Holland Lop, to name a few.

The Pointed White color is also called Californian, as it is found on the breed called by the same name. This same coloration is also called Californian when it is seen on the Rex and Mini Rex.

Completing the picture on white rabbits is the Dwarf Hotot. It, too, is a pure white rabbit, but it has a very fine band of black around the eyes, which are to be a very dark brown. The black eyebands give the rabbit

A blue Beveren. This beautiful color, which can vary in its intensity, can be seen in a number of other rabbit breeds.

Satin Angora. While it is classified as one of the wool rabbit breeds, the Satin Angora is unique because of the shiny, lustrous quality of its wool.

a very unique look, and they are quite attractive.

In addition to the white rabbits, there is a large assortment of other colors available in the various rabbit breeds. The colors are basically divided into three groups. First, there is the Agouti Pattern, in which the body hair shows at least three bands of color—usually alternating dark, light, and dark. The second group is called the Tan Pattern. The trim and markings are the same as in the Agouti, but the body hairs are a solid color—they do not show bands. The third group is called the Self Pattern, in which the rabbit is the same color over the entire body. There are no areas of any other color.

All of the colors seen can be divided into four basic colors: they are black with its dilute counterpart blue, and chocolate with its dilute counterpart lilac. Lilac is best described as a soft dove-gray color and, as in all diluted colors, the eyes are gray.

In addition to the above-mentioned colors and color pattern groups, rabbits also can be found in the "Broken Pattern," which refers to a white rabbit with one or more of the major colors arranged in a breed-specific pattern. The pattern can be spotted, blanket, or patched.

COLOR-RELATED GENES

There are at least ten known series of genes that control the coat color that is seen. How they act and interact with each other produces all of the various colors that we see on all of the known breeds of rabbit.

The Color-Pattern-Setting Genes

These genes control only *where* color will be found on the rabbit.

A: Agouti Pattern—

A young white New Zealand.

American Fuzzy Lops, broken black and sable point.

banded hair shaft.

at: Tan Pattern—solid color body but with typical agouti trim pattern.

a: Self Color—one solid color overall with no markings.

The Color Genes

These genes determine the actual color seen on the rabbit. They will interact with each other to produce a wide spectrum of colors:

B: Black.

b: Chocolate.

C: Full color development.

c(chd): Chinchilla gene—cancels out most of the yellow color.

c(chl): Shading gene—cancels out the rest of

The physical characteristics of a rabbit are determined by its genes, which are received equally from both parents.

the yellow color and also removes some of the black pigment. The "black" then becomes a dark-sepia brown.

c(h): Himalayan/ Pointed White—pure white body, color at the points and always with red/pink eyes.

c: Red-Eyed White— true albino.

D: Dense color and brown eyes.

d: Dilute color and gray eyes.

Es: Steel gene— produces overabundance of dark pigment.

E: Normal extension of dark pigment.

ej: Japanese Brindling gene—produces a mosiac-type color pattern something like tortoiseshell cat coloration.

e: Yellow or red/non-extension of dark pigment.

En: Dominant White Spotting gene—produces a white rabbit with colored areas throughout the coat.

en: Normal color development overall.

Du: Normal color development.

du: Recessive white spotting gene, which is called white-belt. It produces the markings of the

When a breeder is choosing stock for particular characteristics, a basic familiarity with genetics will help to make the job easier and the results more predictable.

Dutch rabbit.
V: Normal coat-color
development with
normal eye color.
v: Vienna White—pure
white body and bright
blue eye color.
W: Normal width of
the agouti band of
yellow or white.
w: Double width of
the agouti band.
Si: Normal color
development.
si: Silvered color.

SOME BASIC RULES OF GENETICS

The dominant gene
in any series is
always listed with a
capital letter, and the
recessive gene(s) are
listed in lower case. If
there are more than
two genes in the
series, another
letter(s) can be added

Silver Marten. The silvering of the fur adds to the overall pleasing appearance of this breed.

to differentiate
between the genes.
They are then listed in
order of dominance,
with the dominant

genes at the top of the list and the most recessive genes at the bottom.

Some dominant genes are completely dominant and will hide the recessive genes when they are present. Other dominant genes will blend with the recessive genes on the series to produce an intermediate effect.

Each living thing can carry only two of the genes from any given series and will pass on only one of them to the sperm or egg. They then join up in the embryo to again have two genes from the series. Littermates may or may not receive the same genes from the parents. It depends on the genes that the parents carry.

For example, if the sire is *Aa* (agouti coated but carrying a recessive self-color gene), he can pass on either the dominant *A* or the recessive *a* to the baby—only one or the other is passed in any one sperm. Some of the babies will get the *A*, and some will get the *a*. If the mother is also carrying the *Aa* combination, she, too, can pass on only one or the other to the baby. The baby then has a 75 percent chance of being agouti coated (*AA* or *Aa*) and a 25 percent chance of being a self-color (*aa*).

EYE COLORS IN RABBITS

Rabbits can have brown, blue, red/pink,

American Fuzzy Lop. Note how the color is lighter on the heavily wooled areas of the body.

or gray eyes. The eye colors are determined by the coat-color genes and do not vary. All densely colored rabbits will always have brown eyes, dilute-color rabbits will always have gray eyes, albino whites and pointed whites will always have red/pink eyes, and Vienna Whites will always have blue eyes.

RABBIT COAT TYPES

There are basically four different types of coats found among the various rabbit breeds. They are the normal coat, the angora coat, the rex coat, and the satin coat.

Belgian Hare. In this breed, the ears are carried in a backward sloping direction.

Netherland Dwarfs, orange and fawn.

The Normal Coat

The normal coat is the type of coat seen on the majority of rabbit breeds. It can be either *fly-back*, which is described as a coat of fur that returns rapidly to its normal position when stroked from rump to head, or it can be *roll–back*, which returns slowly to its normal position when stroked from rump to head. The normal coat is produced by dominant genes and is dominant to all of the other coat types.

The Angora Coat

Over the very long

period of time that rabbits have been kept in captivity, many mutations, or changes, have occurred in the genes for coat type. The most well-known of these mutations and no doubt the earliest to occur is that which gave us the long wooly coat of the Angora breeds. These breeds are raised primarily for their wool, which can be spun into yarn and then made into many different types of clothing articles, e.g., sweaters, gloves, etc.

Because of the length of the wool, the color on the bodies of the long-coated breeds will appear lighter than the same color on the face, feet, and tail. It makes for a beautiful contrast.

The Angora-type coat is found on the English and French Angoras, the Giant Angora, the American Fuzzy Lop, and the Jersey Wooly. This long coat is the result of recessive genes, and a long-coated rabbit bred to another long-coated rabbit will result in all long-coated babies.

The Rex Coat

One of the most fascinating coat mutations is that of the rex coat. This short, plush, and velvety coat was first seen at rabbit shows in Europe in the early 1920s and attracted a great deal of attention from breeders

Opposite: Adult and baby Dutch. The goals of breeders can vary widely. For example, one may wish to improve coat. Another may wish to improve litter size, quicker growth, and so on.

American, blue and white. A breeding pair should complement each other, as their youngsters will carry the combined characteristics of both of them.

and exhibitors. The coat is very short and plush, due to the fact that the guard hairs are just about as long as the hairs of the undercoat. To touch this coat is like stroking velvet. It is very soft and smooth. Like the Angora coat, the rex coat is the result of recessive genes; and a rex-coated rabbit bred to another rex-coated rabbit will always result in rex-coated babies. The rex coat is found on the Rex and Mini Rex breeds.

The Satin Coat

The most recent mutation to come about is the satin coat. It was first found in a litter of Havana rabbits by a breeder in Indiana in 1930. The quickly distinguishable characteristic of the satin coat is its satin-like sheen.

The satin coat is also the result of recessive genes. There are some rabbit breeders that are attempting to produce the satin coat on dwarf rabbit breeds.

The Satin Angora

Sometime after the discovery of the satin coat, breeders interbred satin-coated rabbits with Angora-coated ones to

Netherland Dwarf. Its agouti color resembles that of a rabbit in the wild.

produce the breed known as Satin Angora. The wool of the Satin Angora is finer than that of regular Angora wool; and because of the smaller, thinner hair shaft, which is also transparent, the Satin Angora's coat has a luxuriously rich quality of color. The Satin Angora's coat is also the result of recessive genes.

Editor's note: Due to the constraints of space, this chapter has presented only a general overview of the workings of rabbit coat/color genetics. If you are interested in learning more about this interesting subject, you should visit your pet shop or public library for books written specifically on genetics.

An opal agouti Netherland Dwarf.

Lovely head study of a Satin Angora.

Handling the Mating

A record is made for each rabbit in the rabbitry. This can be done on cards maintained in a card filing box or by keeping a journal or ledger with a page set aside for each rabbit. This record should contain the date of purchase, birthdate, names or identification numbers of the parents, sex, color, breed, and an identification number. There should also be room for making notes for worming dates, illnesses treated, number of young in litters, dates of breedings, and so forth.

Some people prefer to use a hutch card. The hutch card is attached to the outside of the cage and contains information in columns listed as follows: date bred, buck number, date kindled, number of young born (alive–dead), number of young retained, litter number, date weaned, number weaned.

A card for a buck would contain spaces for the identification

Opposite: French Lops mating. In the top photo, the buck mounts the doe. In the bottom photo, the mating has been completed, and the buck falls to the side of the doe.

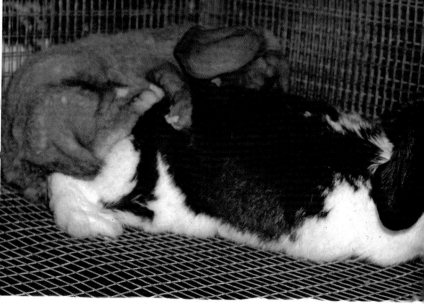

numbers of the does to which he has been bred, the date of the breeding, the number of live young, number of dead young, the date of birth, and the number weaned, as well as the total weight of the litter weaned. This information will tell you at a glance which bucks are producing the quickest-gaining young.

Information from the records can be used to cull stock that is unproductive and to select the desirable animals for future

A litter of Siamese Satins snug and secure in their nestbox. They are one week old.

A Cinnamon. Cinnamons have a normal-type coat, which is seen in most breeds of rabbit.

breeding and improvement programs.

The age to begin breeding depends upon the breed and the individual rate of development. Small breeds develop more rapidly and mature sexually at a much younger age than the medium or large breeds. And some strains within breeds will develop more rapidly than other strains. As a rule of thumb, the smaller breeds can be mated when the bucks and does are five months old, the medium-sized breeds can be bred at six months, and the large breeds at nine to twelve months.

At six months of age, a buck may service one doe a week until fully mature. A mature buck can satisfactorily service one doe a day, or preferably every two days to remain in condition. When a buck is used too heavily, he will lose weight and become unthrifty.

There are several signs to watch for that indicate that the doe is ready for mating. She may become restless and nervous, rub her chin on the feeding and watering containers, or may attempt to join other rabbits in nearby cages. It is not necessary to notice any of these changes in the doe's behavior, because rabbits have no regular heat cycle. They can be bred almost any time. The doe will ovulate six to eight hours after the first mating with the buck. The breeder establishes a working schedule for breeding that fits into his routine and follows that schedule.

The doe to be serviced is always taken to the buck's hutch, and the mating should occur almost immediately. When the mating is completed,

Opposite: Medium-sized breeds can be bred at around six months of age.

A white Mini Lop. This little rabbit is a bit overweight for its size.

the doe is returned to her own cage and a record made of the breeding, noting the date and also the expected date of kindling (count forward 31 days). The identification number of the buck is written on the doe's record, and the identification number of the doe is written on the buck's record. The number of litters a doe can raise depends upon her use. If she is a show rabbit, it is advisable not to raise more than two or three litters a year to maintain her show condition. If the young are to be shown, the mating is arranged so that the litter will be of proper age and development for show classification during the showing season.

Occasionally a doe will not breed. She may be fearful if this is her first mating, or she may be an aggressive

English Spot buck and doe being introduced. Rabbits that are not in tip-top condition will not breed.

doe. In the latter instance, she can be restrained by the handler until the mating is completed.

If the doe is raising litters of young for meat and fur production, she can be bred throughout the year if adequate housing is provided. If the litter is lost at the time of kindling, she can be rebred as soon as the breeder feels it is advisable. A nursing doe can be rebred when the litter

she would become aggressive or refuse service from the buck, and if she were not pregnant, she would be rebred. This is not always an accurate method to determine pregnancy, as some does will accept service when pregnant and others will refuse service when not pregnant.

The only accurate method to determine pregnancy is quick and easy and can be learned by the novice breeder. It is called palpating and is performed between the 12th and 14th day after the mating.

To palpate, place the doe on a flat firm surface. Then, gripping the ears and the skin over the shoulders with the right hand, place the left hand slightly in front of the pelvis between the hindlegs. With the thumb of the left hand on the right side of the doe, and the fingers on the left side, gently exert a slight pressure on the abdomen and move the fingers and thumb backward and forward.

Handle the doe gently, using only the slightest pressure. If the rabbit is pregnant, it is possible to feel the embryos as small hard forms as they slip between the thumb and fingers. After much practice and experience, a breeder becomes accurate at this method. If the

A nice specimen of a black Dutch. The time and planning that go into a breeding program will be reflected in the rabbits that are produced.

handler is inexperienced and unsure of the diagnosis, the doe can be palpated again a week later.

Does that palpate positive are placed on a pregnancy ration and are provided with a nest box on the expected day of kindling. Those that palpate negative should be rebred and palpated a second time.

When colony breeding, whereby six to ten does are kept in a pen on the ground and it is not desirable for the litters to be born in burrows dug by the doe, the does are removed and palpated every ten days. Those that palpate positive are moved to individual cages and given a nest box two days before kindling.

Opposite: Before starting a breeding program, decide what you will do with any rabbits that you might not wish to keep.

Kindling

A day or two before the doe is due to kindle (give birth), a nest box is placed in the cage. If the box is placed within the cage too early, the doe may use it for a toilet. A nesting material of straw, dry grass, or cedar shavings is layered on the bottom of the box to a depth of at least four inches, and preferably six to eight inches if grass or straw is used, as the rabbit mother instinctively tunnels to the bottom, and the material will settle. The doe will investigate the box, rearrange the material to her liking, and begin to make a nest.

Nest boxes are necessary for several reasons. Not only do they keep the young off the wire bottom of the cage and confined for easy care, but also many a newborn rabbit has lost one or more legs when a stray dog discovered it dangling helplessly through wire netting. The exact size of the nest box will depend upon the size of the breed of rabbit raised. The box should be large enough for the doe to make her nest but small enough to discourage her from remaining in the nest once her duties as a

Mixed-breed baby rabbits. Most does give birth during the evening or early morning hours.

mother are performed.

Metal nest boxes can be purchased; or, if the breeder has the extra time and is handy, wood boxes may be constructed of plywood. When the breeder builds his own, they should have three tall sides and a fourth low side. This low side should be low enough to enable the doe to enter and exit with ease, without injury to the udder by bruising. It should also be high enough so that the young do not roll or topple out. If one or more happen to fall out of the box, the doe cannot pick them up and return them to the nest. She is helpless in

Rabbit litters can range in size from around six to eight, and sometimes even larger.

this respect and will nurse only those young remaining in the nest or those that have fallen out of it, not both groups.

The box need not have a top, as moisture may accumulate on the surface and drop back down onto the young rabbits. If the cage is exposed to the elements, a top is preferred; but it should be removable to provide easy access for the handler to inspect the litter. The day of kindling, the doe will act restlessly. She may dig frantically at the bottom of the nest box, arrange and rearrange the bedding to her satisfaction, and will pull fur from her body to line the nest in expectation of her soon–to–arrive litter. Occasionally, a doe will wait until after she

kindles and then quickly pull large amounts of fur to cover the newborns. Most litters are born at night and without complications.

Should the doe deliver her young on the floor of the cage instead of in the nest box, a depression can be formed in the nesting material and the young placed in it. The rabbit keeper can then either pull hair from the doe's body to cover the young or cover them lightly with some of the bedding. The doe will soon discover what her duties are and will enter the box to care for the young.

Baby rabbits are born hairless with a healthy pink color and with eyes and ears sealed. They are most helpless and are born with a jump reflex. This reflex is nature's way of assisting the young rabbit in finding the milk bar. When nursing, the mother rabbit will cover the litter with her body, and the young leap upward to locate her udder.

After the doe has kindled and has left the

Netherland Dwarf nibbling on some garden vegetation.

prove to be too large for the doe to nurse, the surplus young can be moved to the nest of another doe whose litter is of the same age. To do this, a very small amount of a camphor-based ointment is rubbed on each of the baby rabbits, both the ones being added to the nest box and the ones belonging to the foster doe. This way, all the young smell the same, and the doe will accept the new arrivals as her own.

nest, the litter should be inspected. Any dead, deformed, or undersized young are removed. Seven to nine young can be raised satisfactorily by a good milk-producing doe; but should the litter

The biggest hazard to the newborn is chilling. The body's thermostat is not yet working, and the tiny rabbit cannot produce its own heat. The fur the doe pulls to cover her young has

If rabbits are startled or frightened, they will huddle together, just as these Dutch rabbits are doing.

remarkable insulating qualities; the young are warm at birth, and she covers them to retain that warmth. Should one or two of the young become chilled, they can seldom be saved. Chilling occurs when the doe kindles outside the nest box or when temperatures inside the rabbit house drop dangerously low.

There are several methods used to revive young rabbits that have become chilled. The one most practiced by breeders is to place the tiny rabbit in a coat pocket, or better yet, to tuck it inside the coat or shirt front against the warmth of the body. As the handler continues to work in the rabbit house, doing the chores of feeding, watering, and checking on the young in nest boxes, the young rabbit carried against the body receives sufficient heat to revive. When it begins to move and feels warm to the touch, it can be placed with its littermates, making sure it continues to receive heat from those around it.

Another method is the use of an electric heating pad or electric blanket. Overheating is as dangerous as chilling. The temperature setting of the blanket or pad must be at the lowest setting. The chilled rabbit is placed on the pad and covered lightly with a cloth until it is revived and ready to be returned to the litter box.

A well-equipped rabbit house will have heat lamps over the nest boxes or heating units within the boxes. This assures warm quarters even though outdoor temperatures drop below freezing.

When the does are kindling in hot weather, the problem of keeping the young cool is faced. If the young rabbits move away from each other in the nest, this indicates that they are too warm. If the young rabbits spread out, some may not find the doe at nursing time. Remove some of the fur covering them. In extreme heat, all of the covering can be removed.

Most does do not object when the litter is inspected daily if the inspection is done in a quiet, calm manner. However, if the doe appears nervous or aggressive, some tempting treat can be offered to keep her occupied while the young are examined.

In ten or eleven days, the young rabbits open their eyes. Occasionally the eyes of baby rabbits become infected and, instead of opening, remain glued shut. This is due to an infection and can be remedied, if treated promptly, without any permanent eye damage.

A red-eyed white Netherland Dwarf and her youngsters.

To treat the infection, the affected eyes are bathed with a cotton ball and warm water. When the tissue softens, the eye lids are gently separated with the fingertips. If there is pus present, it is wiped away with the cotton ball. An antibiotic ointment or boric acid ointment is applied to the eyes. This treatment is continued daily until improvement is noticed.

Weaning the Young

Being nocturnal, the doe nurses her litter at night or in the early evening and morning hours. As long as the litter remains together, all get fed. But as the youngsters become older and begin to leave the nest, the doe will nurse only those she chooses—either those out of the nest or those remaining in the nest.

The young begin to leave the nest when 19 or 20 days old. They should be fat little fellows. The condition of the young is a good index of the mother's milk capacity. If the young begin leaving the nest sooner than this,

they may not be getting sufficient milk from the mother or the temperature within the nest may be too warm.

By eight weeks of age, the young are eating well on their own and are removed from the doe's cage. Removing the young at this time gives the doe a short rest between litters. If she was rebred when the litter was six weeks of age, she will be pregnant and ready for a rest between litters.

When maintaining a tight breeding schedule, such as in commercial operations where does produce seven or eight litters per year, the doe is bred when the young are 14 days old; the litter is removed from the doe's cage at six weeks of age.

The young rabbits are weighed, and the rapid growers are saved for future breeders, while the slower, underweight individuals are culled. The ideal is to produce litters in which all of the young are close in weight gain. By the time the rabbits are three months old, they should be caged separately to prevent

Rex mother and youngster. Rabbits can be weaned at the age of eight weeks.

fighting and premature breeding.

It is never advisable to keep young that are slow developers for future breeders, or from does that proved to be dirty housekeepers, poor milkers, or of poor temperament. These traits will only carry on through the line in some degree.

ASSESSING THE QUALITY OF YOUR RABBITS

With an increase in the commercial aspect of rabbit raising, breeders have increasingly concentrated their efforts on improving type. Literally thousands of rabbit breeders have banded together to form associations that work toward this goal. Type is more than what is seen on the exterior of a good rabbit. It includes such important qualities as longevity and productivity.

One of the most difficult tasks of the beginner at weaning time is culling the litter. Unless the breeder is an old hand at rabbit raising and is familiar with his line, there is always the possibility of overlooking some good prospect or of keeping a poor one. This is the time when mistakes are made. A good prospect at eight weeks may not look so good at six months. It just did not develop as hoped.

Young bucks can be kept together until they are three months old, after which time they should be housed separately. Does may be kept together for a month longer than this.

There are a few rules of thumb that can be used as a guide in selecting the best of the litter. Look for the individual that is able to put on firm solid flesh and stay firm without putting on a lot of fat. There are rabbits that seem able to do this no matter what is fed to them; their rumps are round and full. If this good smooth rump is not present at weaning time, it never will be.

A youngster should have a good wide loin to balance and support the well-filled rump. There should also be good rib-spread. Rib-spread allows for ample lung room and, as the lungs develop, so will the chest and shoulders. In the young rabbit, a good, flat, broad chest will almost always develop a good set of shoulders. The young littermate possessing a narrow, sharp breast will never improve.

While holding the young rabbit, the breeder places two or three fingers between the front legs and compares several of the young in this manner. It is easy to feel which of the litter have a sharp, narrow chest capacity and which have ample capacity for lung development.

As for head, fur, or ears, it will depend on the particular breed one is raising. It is sometimes difficult to assess fur in the young rabbit, as it still has a soft, immature texture. Several months are required before the full adult coat replaces it enough to judge quality or density. By attending rabbit shows and viewing other rabbits of the same age and breed, the novice breeder will get a pretty good idea of the type to breed for and the type to cull.

The weaned litter is now ready to be recorded separately from the doe. Each individual rabbit that is kept will be given a number and will have its own record, either on a hutch card or in a record book. As a hobby breeder, one strives to

The markings of these mixed-breed rabbits strongly suggest the influence of English Spot genes.

become an authority on his breed, and accurate record keeping allows him to follow the accomplishments of his stock. Experience is the best teacher that one can have, along with talking to other rabbit keepers and generally boning up on research material to be able to select the best from each litter and to guarantee a successful future in rabbits.

Exhibition

By Sheila Hoag

For many rabbit keepers, the highlight of their hobby is exhibiting their rabbits. Adults and children alike take great pride in having their rabbits take show honors. Rabbit shows are held at local and regional levels as well as at the national level.

If you are interested in showing your rabbit(s), the first thing that you should do is contact the national rabbit association for the country in which you live. This organization will provide you with all of the information that you will need to register and show your rabbit.

RABBITS AND 4-H

Some countries have organizations that help to promote the keeping of animals such as rabbits. In the United States, the 4-H organization, whose members range in age from 9 to 19, is quite active in this respect.

Organized in the early 1900s to teach people to grow their crops and livestock better, 4-H has spread across the United States, and more than 70 countries now have similar programs. The 4-H rabbit enterprise, which is what we will focus on here, is just one of more than 40 animal-related

These are just a few of the many ribbons and plaques won by a breeder of lop rabbits. Exhibition is not only interesting and fun but also rewarding and educational.

projects and more than 150 total projects available in 4-H.

4-H is open to anyone who is nine years old by January 1 of the year.

Some areas also provide a mini 4-H program for younger children. There are several different types of memberships to provide for all, and there

A black Silver Marten.

book and member's manual. The record book is turned in to his leader at the end of the year to be evaluated. The manual is a guide book containing helpful information in completing a given project.

The general objectives of a 4-H rabbit project are: to learn better ways to raise your rabbits; to take responsibility for your project; and to maintain accurate records on your rabbits.

For a 4-H rabbit project, a 4-H member selects a breed of his choice. He provides the care and accommodations necessary for the health and well-being of his rabbit. He should also breed his rabbit, raise a

are specialized clubs, as, for example, for rabbits. Your local county extension office can be contacted for information about enrollment.

When a youngster enrolls in a 4-H project, he receives a record

A Holland Lop being judged at a show. The judge will give reasons for the placements of all winners.

litter of young, and make appropriate plans for the offspring that he does not wish to keep. During this whole time, he should keep a detailed record of his rabbit-raising experience, the culmination of which is a rabbit show at the end of the 4-H year.

Members share what they have learned at club meetings. A 4-H rabbit club meeting might include discussion on problems such as how to clear up an outbreak of ear mites; a demonstration on how to groom an

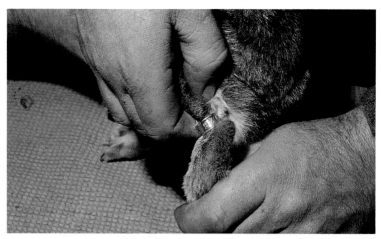

Leg bands are the required means of identification for rabbits that are exhibited in Great Britain.

Angora-type rabbit; and might even include all the members' rabbits for a toenail-clipping session. All members are encouraged to participate and make suggestions for programs. Younger members are given assistance by more experienced 4-H kids, and leaders are there for tough questions.

Some 4-H rabbit clubs are chartered by the ARBA and participate in ARBA-sanctioned county fairs. Other fairs are not ARBA sanctioned, mostly because of size, but the rabbits at such fairs are usually judged by the ARBA Standard of Perfection (breed standards) on a less-strict basis.

THE ARBA CONNECTION

Founded in 1910, the ARBA charters not only state and local rabbit clubs but also national specialty clubs. The ARBA currently has over 50,000 members, many of them 4-H affiliated. It holds hundreds of shows across the country every year.

ARBA judges are required to pass a detailed exam that covers all breeds, varieties, and age groups. A candidate may work as a registrar for years before he becomes a judge, and registrars, too, are tested before they are licensed. With more than 40 breeds of rabbit

involved, becoming a judge can be a time-consuming and tough process. This, however, ensures that the best judges are out there at shows and that rabbit breeders can rely on them.

The ARBA Standard of Perfection is updated and revised every five years. Specialty clubs, that is, clubs specializing in one particular rabbit breed (the National Mini Rex Rabbit Club, for example), write up the original standards for their breeds; these standards are then subject to approval by the ARBA. Once everything is worked out and a final version of the standard is agreed upon, it is set for five years. Updates and changes such as the addition of a new color variety can be voted in by the majority of the specialty club and approved by the ARBA.

A rabbit breeder who wishes to show his stock should obtain a copy of the Standard and study his breed to learn what his objectives should be. The Standard gives acceptable weights, colors, body type, fur type, eye color, toenail color, ear length, head shape, leg and feet type, and bone structure. Since each breed is different, one must research his breed carefully.

Rabbits, as a rule, can be shown at three months of age if they have the potential—that is, good fur, good type, and good condition. Any animal that is sickly, in heavy molt, or within ten days of having babies should not be shown.

Show dates and secretaries are listed in the bi-monthly publication *Domestic Rabbits*, published by the ARBA. Write the secretary and ask to be placed on the mailing list of the clubs in which you are interested in showing. About a month before a show, catalogs are mailed that give details on location, fees, starting time, judges, specialty shows, and rules. There is an entry deadline about a week to ten days before the show. Ninety percent of

Pointed white Jersey Wooly about to be transported to a show. As shows can be stressful, try to make your pet's trips to and from the show as quiet and relaxing as possible.

the shows are held on a Saturday or a Sunday, the exception being county and state fairs.

If for some unforeseen reason a rabbit that you have entered is unable to go to the show, it will be helpful if you inform the show secretary or one of the other people working at the show. This way, the absentee entrant is reported and won't be holding up an entire class.

Most shows are one-day, or basket, shows, again with the exception of county and state fairs.

THE SHOW DAY

Judging generally begins around 8:30 a.m., and there is a midday lunch break. Best in Show is chosen, for the most part, around 4:30 p.m. If a person lives more than a few miles from the show site, he can expect to put in a long day. If an entrant lives two hours away, he must get up around 5:00 a.m. and load his rabbits and other equipment. Then he checks and double checks to be sure that he has the right rabbits and all of the equipment that he needs. Then away he goes to arrive by 8:00 a.m. and to set up. Grooming begins long before the show day,

This Mini Lop is receiving a last-minute touch-up before going to the show bench.

but a final grooming takes place ideally just before the rabbit goes to the judging table.

A list of breeds will be posted at each

variety, is usually called in alphabetical order, although not always.

The judge will carefully examine each animal in turn. He checks to make sure that it is the correct sex and then proceeds to inspect the eyes, toenails, legs, and fur. Teeth are also examined.

Additionally, the judge may weigh the rabbit to be sure that it is the correct weight for its sex, breed, and class. After a rabbit has been inspected, it is returned to its proper space until the judge has looked at the rest of the class.

An underweight or overweight rabbit will be

judge's table. This is the order in which they will be called. Some shows also list the number of entrants in each breed so that the exhibitors can get an idea of when their turn will be. Color, or "washed off the table," that is, eliminated from the competition. An elimination means that the rabbit can be shown at another time, when its problem has been corrected. Other problems that fall into this category include bald spots (in most cases caused by fighting between rabbits in adjacent carrying cages), missing toenails, bad cases of molt, and entry in the wrong class.

If a rabbit is *disqualified*, which means that it has something that makes it unshowable, the judge will state why. It might be an unrecognized color or might have a white spot on otherwise colored fur. Additionally, it might have the wrong eye color or might have a white toenail. This does not mean that the rabbit is useless. If it has good type and only one problem, it can be a very good breeder. Just watch out for those disqualifications in future show prospects.

After the judge has made his first pass, he will go back and begin placing the entrants in order. Each judge has his own system, which exhibitors seldom can figure out unless they watch the same judge over the course of several shows.

When the judge has made his decision, he will begin with the fifth-place rabbit (sometimes he goes

A broken black American Fuzzy Lop. All of the Angora-type rabbits will need extra grooming to keep their lovely wool coats looking their best.

only to fourth place, sometimes up to sixth place). He gives the reason why the fourth-place rabbit was placed as it was, why the third-place rabbit beat the fourth-place rabbit, and so on. Of course, he will also tell why he placed the winner.

After all of the classes for each breed have been gone through in this manner, all first-place winners are required to return to the show table. From them, the judge will choose a Best of Breed for each breed. He goes about this in the same way as he does a regular class. If a doe is chosen as Best of Breed, the judge will pick a buck as Best Opposite Sex. If a buck is chosen as Best of Breed, a doe will be chosen Best Opposite Sex. (In the case in which there is only one sex in competition, there is no opposite chosen.) Later in the show, the Best of Breed winners will compete for the Best in Show, which is awarded at all rabbit shows. Many shows also have a Best 4-class and a Best 6-class. In a Best 4-class, a junior doe, junior buck, senior doe, and senior buck are selected. The larger commercial-type rabbits have six classes: the four just mentioned, plus intermediate doe and intermediate buck. Best 6-classes are also known as 6-8 classes because intermediate-age rabbits are six to eight months old.

In a class of, say, 15 rabbits, each of the 15 owners is sure that his rabbit is best and hopes that the judge will feel the same way. Unfortunately, the judge picks only one winner, which, in his opinion, is the best of the group. Thus, while one owner believes that this is the best judge ever licensed, the other 14 feel as if they have come across a baseball umpire with poor vision! But all is taken in good spirits, the winner congratulated, and the next class called up for a repeat performance.

Don't feel badly if you make a mistake—everyone does. And it's not just the first few times you show. Experienced exhibitors can miss a white toenail, a white spot, or even mistake the sex of their rabbits. (At a national Mini Rex show held in Texas, not one, but *two*, long-time rabbit breeders entered rabbits in the wrong sex classes!)

Nearly everyone has done that; plus, they've experienced a lot of other embarrassing mistakes, but you live and learn.

Once you get home from a show, all of the rabbits that went with you and any new ones that you may have brought home should be quarantined away from the rest of your stock. Even if you seriously doubt that your rabbits could have picked up anything, it's better to be safe than sorry. I know that you've heard that before, but it is true. Also, it is much easier to treat a handful of rabbits rather than every one that you own.

T.F.H. offers the most comprehensive books dealing with rabbits. A selection of significant titles is presented below; they and many other works are available from your local pet shop.

PB-724, 80 pgs, 46 color photos

KW-021, 128 pgs, 127 color photos

CO-0225, 128 pgs, 95 color photos

TW-121, 256 pgs, 109 color photos

H-1073, 128 pgs, 76 color photos

H-984, 320 pgs, 231 color photos

PS-809, 128 pgs, 90 color photos

PS-796, 112 pgs, 75 color photos

SK-001, 64 pgs, 43 color photos

Index